Ghosts of Vietnam:

A Private's Story

By

Michael A. Talerico

Order this book online at www.trafford.com
or email orders@trafford.com

Most Trafford titles are also available at major online book retailers.

Printed in the United States of America.

ISBN: 978-1-4269-2712-6 (sc)

Trafford rev. 11/09/2011

 www.trafford.com

North America & international
toll-free: 1 888 232 4444 (USA & Canada)
phone: 250 383 6864 ♦ fax: 812 355 4082

PRELUDE

It was June 6, 1944; 19-year-old Private Robert John Pepe sits quietly in a "Higgins" boat. The other soldiers also sit quietly while their LCV moves closer to the shoreline. In the distance, they hear the sound of war, shooting, and shelling; heavy artillery and mortars. The smell of gunpowder filled the air.

Omaha Beach was one of the five landing sites of Operation Overlord, the greatest military invasion in the history of mankind. Omaha Beach lost more men on D-Day than the other four beaches combined.

An officer yells out words of encouragement along with instructions to the young men. They are amongst the 2nd wave of the invasion of Normandy, Omaha Beach.

The Higgins Boat hits the shoreline and the front gate drops down into the water. The men start to rush out to the beach.

Machine gun fire is all around them. Mortar rounds are dropping everywhere. Bodies of young American and Allied forces are strewn all over the beach and in the water. Pvt. Pepe scared out of his mind, moves forward watching his comrades being cut down by the Germans.

At the end of the day he is among the survivors.

Two months later, near the city of St. Lo, France, he is involved in a massive attack against a heavily reinforced German army.

He, along with about one hundred and ten allied troops, was wiped out by the German defensive positions.

Pvt. Pepe's body was returned four years later to his hometown of Paterson, New Jersey where he was buried with full military honors. His grave is visited often by his family, especially his sister Theresa.

"I'm falling from the sky. I don't know how it came about, or where I was falling from, but I was falling and nothing was going to stop me from crashing into the ground." This was a recurring dream I had as a small child, and this was to become my biggest fear.

One day when I was a teenager, my father and my older brother, Bill, went up to the roof of our home to repair our television antenna.

Out of curiosity, I followed them.

About 6 or 7 rungs up the ladder I realized something was drastically wrong.

I was higher than I had ever been and I was petrified. My arms were wrapped around the ladder with a death grip.

Going further up was not an option.

Slowly I started down the ladder, very cautiously, one rung at a time.

Stepping off the ladder back onto the ground was a great relief.

Never again would I dare anything involved with height, or so I thought.

DEDICATION

This book is dedicated to the men who died in Vietnam and to those who returned wounded. It is also dedicated to the men who returned home unscathed only to find indifference towards their efforts.

They have no medals, no visible wounds; they are the real heroes of Vietnam because for them the war has never ended. They were not volunteers. Their country required them to serve.

They suffer the wounds of a nation that made them feel unloved, "Fore no greater love a man can give his country than to lay down his life for it". Although they were prepared to do just that, they survived.

No medals, no wounds, just the memory of what they gave.

For Robert John "Bobby" Pepe, the uncle I never knew.

For Roberta Kwiatkowski, my mother-in-law, who upon hearing some of the stories, convinced me to put them in writing. Without her encouragement at the beginning I never would have started it.

And for my grandchildren, who, without this book, would never truly know their grandfather.

And for my son, Willy.

For Andrew

During my lifetime I had witnessed and
have heard about acts of courage, from
firemen rushing into burning buildings,
soldiers sacrificing their lives for their
comrades, and policemen risking their
lives to protect the innocent.

Courage comes in many ways. Usually
when you least expect it.

How you handle a hardship is one of the ways that requires the
most courage. When things seem to be the worst, when you feel
you have nothing left, that all is lost, is when a person's level of
courage is tested the most.

I would like to give a special dedication to my cousin Andrew
Thomas Quinn, who at the tender age of thirteen has shown me
what courage truly is.

Andrew has been diagnosed with Bone Cancer and has to endure
nine months of intense chemotherapy.

He has challenges ahead of him no one should have to endure,
but he is handling it with strength and honor not often seen in
men, let alone a teenager.

He will be well and he will do something special with his life. He is
a remarkable boy.

His courage has given me the strength and commitment to finish
this story. If anyone asks me "what was the biggest motivation for
finishing this book", I would tell them in a heartbeat, "Andrew
Quinn. I did it for him."

Thank you, Andrew

Acknowledgements and Contributors

Jo Gosman
Bill Talerico

Editors:
Mary Yurkosky
Ron Mineo
Bill Talerico

Contributors:
J. Michael Deems
Steve Becsei
Roger Bray
Lowman Abraham
J.D. Corbett

This book is a collection of memories from my experience in the military. The names and dates are true as best I can remember, and estimated when I can't. The only combat situations are those that had a direct impact on me.

The stories are true.

Many men who have served their country faithfully will relate to these stories. I was there and I know them to be true.

When you see the names on the "Wall", you begin to remember that it was not a joke.

We gave all we had, and used the stupid events and attitudes that I describe in this book to hide our fears and tears.

THE INSPIRATION

Going Nowhere

Fresh out of high school, I was working in a small diner in Little Falls, NJ. I was the cook, dishwasher, waiter, and busboy. The time was February 1965.

I barely made it through high school, mainly due to the fact that I had a lot of trouble staying awake in class. I thought back then that I was tired all the time, but now realize that it was boredom.

It was also when I realized that I had a serious problem with authority figures, especially when their authority was aimed at me. Needless to say, I wound up doing what my education prepared me for, short order cook.

But I was damn good at it.

One afternoon, while getting ready to close the diner, I heard a song on the radio that changed my life.

It was a song that I had not heard played on the radio ever. It hit me like a ton of bricks.

The diner was empty and my work was near completed, so I just listened. It was a long ballad, one that I have heard many times, but never like this.

I started getting goose bumps all over from the music. My heart started racing, it was like a message being sent directly to me. I knew exactly what it meant.

As soon as I got off from work, I got on the bus to Paterson, NJ and went downtown to the Selective Service center.

I walked inside and went right up to the person at the front counter

and asked where do I sign up?
I wanted my name placed at the top of the draft list.

I was patriotic, but this way I would only have to serve 2 years, joining meant 3 or 4 years.

I signed some papers and was out of there.

I never said a word to anyone about that day. The song was "The Battle Hymn of the Republic." Till this day I get a lump in my throat and goose bumps whenever I hear it.

The following month I received "Greetings" from the President of the United States. I was to report for active duty April 13, 1965.

BASIC TRAINING

The Eve of Induction

The night before my induction into the army, my older brother Bill and I were sitting in the den of our parents' home talking about my next 2 years.

We really didn't talk much together except for the normal sibling arguments. He is 3 years older and I was the "little" brother who was always in the way.

But this night was different. He wasn't teasing me or criticizing me in any way. I detected a certain amount of respect rarely, if ever, shown to me by him.

He said something that got me thinking. "If you are going to be in the Army for 2 years, why not do something that you would probably never do otherwise, like be a ranger or better yet, a paratrooper."

I thought about what he said and even though it was never going to happen because of my acrophobia, the thought of being a paratrooper started to intrigue me.

The Induction

Joining the Army was the first time I was ever on my own. I didn't even go to summer camp like other kids, so this was it. No parents to protect me, no friends to stand by my side in the face of trouble, no big brother to jump in if the going got rough.

I was looking forward to it. I wasn't looking to kick ass like a lot of other guys wanted, I just wanted to get in and get out, and maybe do something different.

When the bus from Paterson arrived at Fort Dix, NJ, it was at night. The weather was damp and cold. People were walking around all over the place.

We were taken to an area where many soldiers were marching this way and that way. Guys in military overcoats, long hair, and confused looks on their faces were standing around like they didn't know what to do or where to go.

Someone in our group said they were officers because they didn't have any stripes. I didn't think much about them, instead I was thinking about what my brother had said the night before.

It stuck in my head and I couldn't think of anything else.

He was my big brother, who I had always envied. The thought of doing something that would impress him and make him proud of me was becoming almost an obsession.

I was his little brother who always tagged along. This was my chance to be his buddy. The only problem with being a paratrooper was that it was high up in the air and you had to jump out of an airplane, which   I could never do.

Other than that it sounded pretty cool.

Soon after, we were shuffled into a tent like barracks. There we were given some clothing and one of those military overcoats.

Now I understood who those guys with no stripes were, they were on the bus before us. I had met some guys who were in line with me and we started talking.

One of them said they were going outside to mess with the next busload of recruits.

While we were waiting for instructions, a few of us went outside to watch what was going on.

We stood near the guys waiting for the buses. When the next bus pulled up we were ready.

As the recruits got off the bus we started giving out orders. One of the guys I was with started yelling at some kid. He got all over this kid, giving him orders like he was a four-star general.

He even had some of them drop down to the ground and do pushups. We could barely keep a straight face. After all, we thought the guys in the overcoats were officers at first ourselves.

Later that evening, we saw some other guys in overcoats doing the same thing.

Shots

The Army had an interesting way of administering the necessary medical shots needed. Medics formed 2 lines about 5 feet apart.

They faced each other forming a gauntlet. We, the unsuspecting recruits, had to walk at a slow pace through this gauntlet while the medics would shoot us in each arm with their guns.

One would think the situation called for medical professionalism and concern for the patient. Well, not here.

The medics were shooting at our arms, across the gauntlet at the other medics, down the line at recruits, in the back of the head of passing recruits, and anywhere else their hearts desired.

Guys were coming through the line with blood dripping down their arms. Some fainted, other screamed, and a few ran out of there. In the end, I had received 8 shots in about 20 seconds.

Oscar Company

Fort Dix was a place I had never heard of before. It is an old Army base located in southern New Jersey and is next to Maguire Air Force base.

I knew I was going to spend the next 8 weeks there, and thought it was   going to be the toughest 8 weeks of my life.

 I was assigned to "O" company. The "O" stood for "Oscar." It was the first time I heard the word "Oscar" used for the letter "O". I thought then that it was a stupid organization that would place a group of would-be killers in an outfit called "Oscar."

I was assigned to the 1st platoon. Our platoon leader was a staff sergeant named S/Sgt. Lawrence Pauciello.

Sgt. Pauciello took us inside our barracks and got right to the point. We do what we are told and nobody gets messed with. Make him look bad and we are dog meat.

Sgt. Pauciello had a CIB (Combat Infantry Badge) and a combat patch, and was constantly telling us "you will die on the battlefield of a remote jungle unless you pay attention now."

While we were inside listening to him, the other 2 platoons were outside getting screamed at by their platoon sergeants, Sgt. Hoskins and Sgt. Pesta. I knew then that I had lucked out and got a pretty cool sergeant.

So did the rest of the platoon.

Sgt. Pesta

Sergeant Pesta ran the 2nd Platoon. He had a Smokey the Bear hat and between his chinstrap and the bottom of his hat was nothing but pure mean.

He was about 5 feet 10 inches tall and around 190 pounds. He was always belching out orders to his platoon. They couldn't get anything right according to him.

They were maggots, pond scum, and worthless pieces of garbage. His platoon hated him with a passion. He worked his platoon day and night.

We would be hanging out in our barracks and see out the windows how he worked his platoon. They worked their marching drills at least 3 times more than we did.

We would be in a company formation and he would be the only Platoon Sgt. yelling at his platoon. He made it very clear to his platoon that they would win the marching drill at the graduation ceremonies at the end of basic training even if it killed them.

Sgt. Pauciello would have us march every day, but he instructed us when we messed up rather than yelling.

Don't get me wrong, I did my share of push-ups, but not like mad dog Pesta.

Occasionally, when an officer was near, Sgt. Pauciello would yell a little but we knew it was only for show.

If there was someone having trouble, the rest of us would practice on our own time with them. We actually started looking pretty good.

Sgt. Pesta continued his extra drills right up to the end. We were looking forward to graduation.

The Ballantine

I didn't realize it until I entered the Army, but I never had a toy gun of any kind. I learned later on that it had to do with my uncle being killed in WWII.

This was going to be the first time I fired a weapon. Not a toy, but a U.S. Army M-14 rifle. We would go out to the rifle range a few times each week and practice firing our weapon.

We fired several different types of weapons, but the main training was the M-14. The goal everyone tried to reach was to score a "Ballantine"; this was the result of having three rifle shots overlap each other forming   a hole, which resembled the Ballantine Beer symbol.

I was pretty good with my rifle and I was consistent with hitting the target from different ranges.

After 4 weeks in basic we were allowed to have weekend passes if we earned it. I wanted to get a pass for the weekend and asked Sgt. Pauciello if I could have one.

He made me an offer, get a Ballantine and I get the pass. Nobody from any of our platoons had gotten one so far and I wasn't the best riflemen by any means.

We had guys who were hunters who were considered the better riflemen, but I really wanted the pass.

The rest of the week I concentrated on what I was taught and the following week I scored Oscar's one and only Ballantine for the entire 8 weeks of basic.

I still have the target with the little Ballantine Beer symbol.

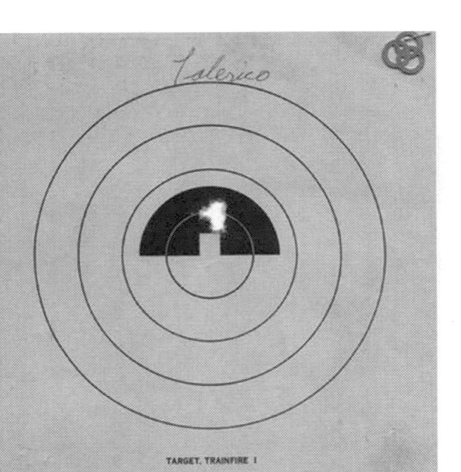

TARGET, TRAINFIRE I

First Article 15

I was never one for doing something dirty or dangerous if I could avoid it. So far I'd missed the crawling under machine gun fire, the 20-mile hike, and most of the other hazardous training operations.

I thought my ass was cake. I was able to easily handle these "lifers" like a fine tuned violin. Piss them off just a little, at the right time, and those morons would slap a detail on me before they realized that they just got me out of another exercise.

I felt if I could avoid it now, I could avoid it later. Unfortunately, my luck ran out.

One day I was avoiding one of those hazardous training exercises by "volunteering" for some detail in the company area, however, I made a big mistake.

Thinking everyone was gone for the day; I finished my detail early and sneaked back into the barracks for a nap. I had about 3 hours before anyone would come back.

Not long after I was awakened by a loud thud.

It was my head hitting the floor complements of the 2nd platoon sergeant, Sgt. Pesta. He started screaming something at me, I couldn't make it out, but I got the message.

As I was backing up from his screaming I found myself backing into the company commander's office.

There I met the company commander face to face.

He introduced me to my 1st Article 15, the Army's version of a speeding ticket.

Normally, your pay would be cut in half, but since I made the minimum ($39 per month) that didn't happen. I also would have lost one rank, but again, being a buck private, nothing happened there either. I got off pretty easy considering.

From that point on I became very careful not to mess up like that again.

As far as Sgt. Pesta was concerned, he would get his real soon. Airborne

We would start each day by doing physical training. Sit-ups, pushups, squat thrusts, jumping jacks, and in the end we would run.

We also went to the rifle range, and other outdoor activities.

In between we would have classes, some on health, others on first aid, and the list goes on.

Sometimes we would go to an auditorium where people from different parts of the Army would come to try and recruit us into their group.

This day we had a visit from the airborne representative. The speaker was an old time sergeant who kept belching when he spoke.

Each time he belched, he held his stomach and would say "Mary's Bar" like that was cool. I thought he was an idiot, like we should be impressed because he drinks. But he was talking about the airborne and all I could think of is what my brother said.

Even though I knew I would never actually do it, I went ahead and signed up for the airborne just to see how far I could go.

Confidence Course

As we neared the end of basic training, we were brought to the obstacle or confidence course. This was a pretty easy course to run.

Jump through some tires, go hand over hand across monkey bars, climb a rope that had knots every few feet.

You had to be in pretty bad shape not to breeze through this course. I had no problem with everything they had.

Then, Sgt. Pauciello called me over and told me to go with a small group to another part of the course.

This was the group of guys that had signed up for the airborne. We marched over to what appeared to be a big ladder, not my favorite thing.

We were told to climb up the ladder and then at the top, go over the ladder and climb back down.

This ladder was about 30 feet in the air. The 2 sides were about 8 feet apart and the rungs were like 6 x 6's. A few guys started up the ladder and I thought, here goes, and followed them up the ladder.

It wasn't too bad, I wasn't afraid of the height. The rungs were only a few feet apart.

Then something happened that got me a little worried. The higher I went, the further apart the rungs were.

Eventually, the rungs were further apart than I was tall. Some of the guys shimmied up the end posts to the top. I moved over to attempt it but I found myself with a death grip on the post.

Sgt. Pauciello yelled from the ground, "Get over that top if you want to go airborne". Maybe he threw in a few expletives, I can't remember.

I looked at him, I looked at the top rung, and then I proceeded to climb back down, nice and slow.

When I reached the ground Sgt. Pauciello came over and asked me what happened. I told him that I just went higher than I ever did in my life. He just laughed.

Most of the other guys didn't make it over the top, but a few did. Airborne wasn't looking too good at this point.

Graduation

The 8th week finally came and the ceremonies were about to begin. Sgt. Pesta had his platoon training day and night. He wanted to win this competition real bad.

No one understood why he was so obsessed with winning.

The 3rd platoon and ours didn't train half as much as the 2nd platoon. We just assumed that they would win the drill competition, and we couldn't care less if they did.

This morning was no different. Bright and early Sgt. Pesta had his platoon marching all over the company area. They marched while we went to breakfast, after breakfast, and right up to company formation.

After breakfast Sgt. Pauciello sat with us in the barracks and gave us all words of encouragement, last minute tips, and told us we were good enough to win. "Just do your best. Do what you have been taught and the rest will come."

He told us that there would be a number of companies graduating and not to worry.

We all liked him, even more than we despised Sgt. Pesta. When the ceremonies were completed, we won 1st place, and Sgt. Pesta's platoon came in 7th or 8th, and it was beautiful.

We then watched Sgt. Pauciello walk over to Sgt. Pesta and collect what seemed to be money. On his way back to our platoon we all cheered him, making sure Sgt. Pesta heard us.

We loved it.

This was the end of basic training, which was supposed to be the hardest
part of the Army. I didn't lose any weight; however, I was in a little

better shape.

The main thing I learned was how easy it was to get around things I didn't want to do.

The Army was a piece of cake and I was going to slide through the next 2 years. I was in like Flint.

ADVANCED INFANTRY TRAINING

After Basic Training, I returned home for a month long leave. The ordeal of basic training had little effects on me. I weighed about the same, a little firmer though.

My attitude was as bad as it was in high school, perhaps worse. I thought for sure the Army would straighten me out. I spent the last 8 weeks learning how to scam the NCOs (Non Commissioned Officers), to be the one who gets that lousy detail, only to miss some dangerous or difficult training exercise.

I thought my ass was cake. I was able to easily handle these "lifers" like a fine tuned violin. Piss them off just a little, at the right time, and those morons would slap a detail on me before they realized that they just got me out of another exercise.

Now I was heading to Fort Gordon, Georgia. This time I had to spend another 8 weeks in something they called AIT. No one knew exactly what AIT meant.

Some thought it was Advanced Infantry Training; others thought it was Airborne Infantry Training, because all the guys in it were given an airborne MOS (Military Occupation Specialty). Either way, it sucked.

I found a higher quality of NCO. They were prepared for the likes of us, especially me.

All of a sudden I found myself in the real Army. No more details for discipline, extra laps around the track was the usual penalty for mouthing off or just looking at them the wrong way.

I spent a lot of time at the beginning running around the track, so much so that I got pretty good at running.

For the next 8 weeks we all worked our tails off. Physical training was push-ups, sit-ups, jumping jacks, squat thrusts, and finally running.

This was done every morning at 5:30 am. After PT was mess. There we had about 30 minutes to get our food and eat it.

After mess was training. Like basic, this consisted of classes, hikes, and rifle range, and more running.

The drill instructors would take turns leading us. Those old bastards could run forever, at times it seemed like they would never stop.

They enjoyed watching us suffer. It was like them showing us how pathetic we were.

Fortunately, I had developed into a pretty good runner myself. Little did I know how I would use that to my advantage a little later on.

I learned to stay out of trouble. These NCOs did not fool around and I ran enough already.

Scams were a thing of the past; I had no choice but to follow directions and keep my mouth shut. I stayed clear of any problems.

The NCOs hardly knew who I was, and I liked it like that.

Physical Training Test

At the end of AIT, a physical training test is given to determine who will continue on to Jump School at Fort Benning, Georgia.

Cadre from another outfit administered the test. Our sergeants were not even there so there was no favoritism.

This was the "test" that lets you know if you are "Airborne" material.

It sounded pretty easy; 22 push-ups, 8 pull-ups, 50 sit-ups in two minutes, some squat thrusts in a few minutes, and for the finale, you had to run a mile in eight minutes.

Sounds easy? Wrong, the push-ups had to be perfect, body completely straight or they wouldn't count. Start in a prone position then go down to one inch from the ground, hold it one second, then go completely up, hold one second, and repeat.

Some guys had to do 60 push-ups in order to get 22 perfect ones. Pull-ups were even harder. First of all, they were overhand, start from the bottom, all the way down.

Pull up over the bar and hold for one second, then go down all the way and hold for one second, repeat. This is where a lot of guys failed.

Fortunately for me, my friend Mike Chirichella from high school and I would compete in gym class every day. We both got to be pretty good at pull-ups.

Who knew it would come in handy. This was the hardest part of the test along with the run. The sit-ups and squat thrusts were not too bad.

The run, one mile in eight minutes sounded okay, except for one thing. We were wearing boots and fatigues. It was August in

Georgia and hot and humid. Pacing myself, I was able to complete it in about 6 ½ minutes.

I completed the test in good shape and was pleased with my performance.

I went back to my barracks after the test and all I wanted was a shower and to rest. However, when I arrived at my barracks, a friend of mine, Joe, was sitting on his bunk with his head in his hands.

He was upset about something. When I asked him what was wrong, he told me he couldn't do the push-ups or the pull-ups. He wanted to go "Airborne" more than anything and didn't know what to do. I figured, "What the hell" I would do the test for him.

They constantly hammer into our heads about the "Buddy system" so here was my opportunity. I told him to give me his fatigue shirt and his ID number and off I went.

There were about 500 people taking the test, all with the same haircut and clothes. What were the odds of anyone recognizing me? I took the test a second time. It was harder, but I still made it thru okay.

Again I went back to my barracks, really needing a shower. I gave Joe his shirt back and congratulated him on going "Airborne".

He was my friend forever or at least thru the rest of AIT.

While I was getting ready for my overdue shower, another guy, who knew what I did, asked me if I would take the test for him.

He wasn't anyone I hung around with, and I was tired, so I declined. He then offered me $20 to take his test.

I took the test a third time. This time some of the things I did were not counted so it started to get to me. I wanted to quit, but something inside of me kept telling me to go on.

About half way through the run I started to cramp up. I started walking, hoping to get a second wind, or in this case, a fourth wind.

My watch showed 7 minutes had gone by and I still had about a quarter mile to go. I don't know where it came from, but I started double-timing the rest of the way.

I finished the mile in 7:53. 7 seconds to spare.

Jump School, here we come.

JUMP SCHOOL

Fort Benning, Georgia

Ft. Benning, Georgia is the home of the Airborne Jump School. The school lasts three weeks, how hard could it be? I was in great shape and ready for anything, well almost anything.

I assumed that this would be the end of my quest for the impossible, actually jumping out of an airplane. Just the thought of it made me quiver with fear. I don't know why I even bothered going this far, it entailed extra training, harder work, less sleep, and more gung ho bullshit.

As I entered the main gate at Ft. Benning, I saw a sign that read "Ft. Benning, Home of the Airborne". That was the first time I had actually seen anything that had to do with the "Airborne", other than the idiot Sgt. at basic training.

This time I got goose bumps. "Wouldn't it be cool if I actually jumped out of an airplane?"

The first day of jump school was enlightening; some officer came out to address our company formation. He spoke for a few minutes about how the "Airborne" was the elite force of the army, etc., etc., and then disappeared, never to be seen again until graduation.

Then came "Smokey." "Smokey" was the name given to the cadre. They were the Sgts. that were to train us.

They were all about one hundred and sixty pounds, lean, and mean. They got the name by wearing the Smokey the Bear hat, same as basic and AIT, only this time they were louder than the cadre at basic and smarter than the cadre at AIT.

We were told that there were twelve hundred in our class; however, only three hundred would be graduating in three weeks.

There was to be no talking while in training, in line at the mc33 hall, or while traveling to different areas of the base.

If you got caught talking, you were out, no second chance. If you created any kind of problem, no matter how minor, you would ave to drop and knock out ten push-ups.

Smokey wouldn't fire you, but he would make you want to quit. Ten push-ups was a joke, I thought.

Smokey told us that army rules are no more than ten push-ups at one time. There must be at least one other order in between the sets of push-ups. So, if he wanted to, Smokey would have you drop, knock out ten, when you stand back up he would give you a command such as "About face", then drop and do ten more.

This could go on as long as he liked. If you couldn't do any more push-ups, he would have you run.

Another requirement was that when you completed your push-ups you were to jump to attention and say "Thank you Sergeant Airborne".

We had a few marines and one guy from the navy's Underwater Demolition Team or UDT. They kept to themselves for the most part.

In three weeks or less I would know whether or not I could overcome my fear of height.

I wasn't too pleased with my brother at this point.

The First Week

I thought jump school was about jumping out of airplanes, how to jump, fall, and land. That was it. What else could it be?

Jump school was more push-ups, sit-ups, squat thrusts, and my favorite, running. Every day we ran and ran and ran. In between running we did exercises. Oh there were a few classes here and there, but week one was exercise.

Smokey would pick on someone for a while, just to see if they could take it. If they could, he left them alone and moved on to someone else.

If you had to drop, then you better do the push-ups perfect and yell loud and clear upon completion "Thank you Sgt. Airborne". That was the best way to stay out of Smokey's way.

It was September in Georgia, and very hot and humid. One day, around 2:00 pm, Smokey walked over to the UDT and said something. The UDT made the mistake of answering him.

Smokey told him to drop because he spoke in formation. The UDT, to everyone's surprise, asked Smokey which arm he would like him to use.

This was not a smart thing to say, no matter how physically fit you are. Smokey walked up to the UDT, about an inch from his face, and said,
"Use both arms".

The UDT got down, completed his ten push-ups and jumped to attention and yelled "Thank you Sgt. Airborne UDT".

He was testing Smokey, not a good idea. Smokey ordered him to "about face", and then knock out ten more. The UDT repeated his push-ups and again jumped to attention yelling "Thank you Sgt. Airborne UDT".

Smokey's ego was being pushed to the limit. We all were standing at ease, but were nervous that Smokey would take his anger out on us.

This went on for about eighty push-ups. Smokey soon realized that this UDT could go on forever. He ordered the entire company to attention.

While we stood at attention, in the hot afternoon sun, Smokey told the UDT to get in the prone (the up part of a push-up) position and stay in the prone position, without moving, until he sees three drops of sweat fall from his nose. The UDT got down and was motionless while in the prone position.

While he was down on the ground, Smokey proceeded to tell us about how many years he has been in this man's army. How he has seen every type, and how no one has ever beaten him in jump school.

He explained how different people have tried, even gave some examples,
but mainly he was just passing time talking.

Every once in a while he would look over at the UDT to see if he was sweating from his nose yet. He would walk over to the UDT and lean down and say things like "We have all afternoon, so take your time".

We were all sweating just looking at this poor guy, but he was not going to quit.

After about twenty minutes, Smokey saw a drop of sweat forming on the UDT's nose. He got right down to view the first occurrence of sweat dropping.

All of a sudden Smokey jumped up and announced in a loud and clear voice, "One". The first drop of sweat fell to the ground.

Finally! The next two should come soon.

After another five minutes or so the second drop fell, and again the announcement. A few minutes later the third and final drop of sweat fell from the UDT's nose at which point he feebly jumped to attention and yelled "Thank you Sgt. Airborne".

Smokey had won. We never heard another word from the UDT again. He met his match.

At the end of the week we were informed that too many people had made it to this point, so today was going to be a little harder. More people had to quit.

Near the end of the day we were told that we had fifty people more than allocated to move on to the next week.

Smokey informed us that what we were going to do was run around the track until fifty people dropped out. I wasn't too worried; I did pretty well at running. So we started to run around the track.

After several laps some guys dropped out. A few more laps and some more dropped out. Then Smokey announced that they needed five more to drop out before we could stop running.

I was getting tired and was getting worried that I might not make it. So I got an idea. I fell to the back of the group where some guys were struggling to keep up.

I started talking, quietly of course, to the last guy. I said things like "You don't look so good, are you all right?" and "Hey, it isn't worth a heart attack, you look white", even to the black guys.

This worked, one at a time they just gave up. I felt a little guilty for doing it, but they weren't going to make it anyway, why prolong the agony.

Smokey got his fifty and we all were done with week one.

The Second Week

Well, I made it through week one. It was hell, all we did was exercise, and more exercise. Week two was the beginning of our actual jump training.

We started each day with exercising in the morning before mess. But after we ate breakfast, we started doing some interesting things.

We were taught how to land on the ground. The first thing we were taught was to relax as we descend, and to keep our knees bent slightly.

When we hit the ground we were to land with a twisting motion, first the bottom of our toes, then the balls of our feet, then our calves, still twisting, then our thighs, followed by our buttocks and finally our backs. This is called a "Parachute Landing Fall" or better known as a "PLF".

We were taken to a four-foot wall with sand on the ground in front of it. After being shown how to do it, we took turns jumping on the sand and practicing our PLF's. We had to land sideways to the right. We also landed to the left and even backwards.

There were a few lines moving to different parts of the wall so we each had several opportunities to practice. All the while Smokey was yelling at us, having us drop for stupid reasons, anything to make us quit.

Next was learning what it is like hanging from a parachute. Here we were taken inside a barn type building and introduced to what is lovingly called the "Nutcracker".

There were several harnesses hanging from the ceiling via pulleys. We were strapped into them and pulled up a few feet off the ground. The harnesses were wrapped around both legs, up over the groin, and around the shoulders.

After being pulled up off the ground we soon realized how it got its name. We hung for about five minutes before being taken down.

Only a couple of guys couldn't jump off the four foot wall, and a few more weren't able to sustain the nutcracker, but the next part would be the number one reason people quit jump school, and my biggest fear, the thirty-four foot tower.

The thirty-four foot tower looks like a guard tower you see in the movies. It had a stairway going up to a platform with walls and a roof. On one side of the platform was an opening about the width of an airplane door.

One at a time, someone was strapped into a harness. Outside the tower, on the side by the door was a cable that ran from the left of the tower door about a hundred feet to the right of the tower.

An eight-foot strap to the cable outside of the tower attached the harness we were strapped in. At the end of the cable was a mound of dirt where another trainee was prepared to catch you and unhook the harness.

As soon as he would unhook the harness, the rope man, another trainee, was to run at his top speed, sliding the harness back to the tower.

This was repeated for each trainee. This was where most guys just up and quit. Looking down from the door of the thirty-four foot tower was a psychological terror. More people feared jumping from the tower than from an airplane.

As I moved up the staircase I was telling myself I couldn't do this. Here was my limit, I was unable to jump from the tower and I hadn't even seen the top of it yet.

But then something happened that made me move on. As we were slowly moving up the tower, some guys were coming down the stairway. They were the ones who couldn't do it. They quit because of their fear. I didn't want to be one of them.

I started thinking about how far I've come and if I quit, I would always regret it. It was something I didn't want to live with. The fear of quitting, especially at this point, was greater than the fear of jumping off this tower. How could I look my brother in the eye ever again?

I started to think how no one had gotten hurt so far, a lot of guys were jumping off successfully. Why not me? If I were the only one on the tower I would have quit, but because there is strength in numbers I continued up the stairway.

In the meantime, the rope man, which was the worse job in the school, was busy running back and forth. Every time he brought the harness and rope back to the tower Smokey would tell him he was too slow and make him drop and do ten push-ups. This job was given to anyone who got in Smokey's way.

It was too hard for most of the rope men, and compounded with having to do the push-ups and putting up with the verbal abuse, about half of them quit.

I was now at the top of the tower. It was high, a lot higher than thirty-four feet, about a hundred feet, or so it seemed. There were four guys in front of me.

The first guy got strapped in and jumped with no problem. The next guy walked up to the edge before he strapped in and turned around and walked back down the stairs. The third jumped. Then the fourth guy jumped.

Now it was my turn. I strapped into the harness, stood up to the door, and while quietly praying jumped to what was impending doom.

To my relief, I felt a yank and I started sliding to the dirt mound at the end of the cable. I was relieved that I was able to get by the tower.

The next thing to accomplish was jumping from the two hundred foot tower.

The two hundred foot tower was originally from Coney Island, NY. You were strapped into a harness with a parachute, pulled up to the top of the tower, and then dropped.

Unlike Coney Island, you were not connected to anything on your way down. For some reason this didn't bother me. After all, it was a ride at an amusement park.

The first guy hooked up and was pulled up to the top. When he was released, the wind, which was kicking up a bit, took him across our area over to the OCS (Officers Candidate School) parking lot where he landed safely.

After that, the rest of the training was cancelled. I never got to jump from the two hundred foot tower, and that was okay with me.

At the end of week two, we were again over our allotted amount of trainees, so we had to go back to the track. This time I started at the back of the group. I wasn't going to wait until I was near exhaustion, I wanted to start early. I would run alongside the last guy and talk to him. I usually started with words of encouragement, followed by words of concern about his health. It worked again; the required amount of guys dropped out and week two was complete.

The Third Week

The third week of jump school was about actually jumping out of an airplane. This was it. No walls, no towers, just you and the airplane.

Exercise was limited to the mornings, which was a relief.

Our first jump was on Monday. We went to the airbase at Ft. Benning. We were then given a parachute with a reserve.

We were instructed to keep our right hand on the D-ring of the reserve at all times.

This was important because if your main chute didn't open you had to pull your reserve and you didn't want to go looking for the D-ring while plummeting to the ground. So everyone got their chute.

With our right hand on our D-ring we walked across the airstrips where the planes were waiting. It was around 1:00 pm, and another scorcher of a day.

It was a long walk across the airstrip, but we finally made it to the planes. We were told to sit on the ground until it was our turn to board the next plane.

While sitting on the ground in the hot sun, I started wondering what I was doing here. This was no longer AIT, where there were no planes involved. Even the first two weeks of jump school had the security of knowing that there were no planes involved.

But now there are planes and I'm sitting on the ground waiting to climb into a plane with the sole purpose of jumping out of it at a great height. "What am I doing here? Am I out of my mind?"

I'll never forgive my brother for making that stupid suggestion in the first place. If he didn't say anything, I would be a supply clerk somewhere safe. I began to hate the bastard.

A sergeant walked by me, as I raised my right hand to get his attention. He saw me raise my hand and immediately walked up to me and pulled my unprotected D-ring. My reserve chute popped out of its casing and dropped in front of me, I should have used my left hand.

He told me if I wanted a new reserve, I had to double time over to the hanger where we got our chutes and get another reserve. I immediately started running to the hanger.

As I was running, the thought of not making it back to the plane on time for the jump started going through my mind. If I'm too slow I would miss the jump. This could be my out. If I didn't make it back in time I would probably be cut, not for chickening out, but for being late.

I found myself not slowing down because I knew it would have been because I was afraid to jump. Again, that seemed to be my driving force. I began running faster, making sure I got back in time.

I reached the hanger, received another reserve chute and ran back as fast as I could. As soon as I got back, with my right hand firmly holding my new D-ring, we started loading into the plane.

We entered into the back of the plane forming two lines. One line went to the seats on the left side of the plane and one line went to the seats on the right side of the plane.

Unlike commercial airlines, the seats were made of cloth straps on a metal frame. They folded up to the side of the plane, or down for sitting. We sat in our seats and the plane started down the runway.

This was it. The moment of truth had arrived. Boy was I scared. I wasn't the only one. Some were quietly praying. Some were being loud and obnoxious, while hiding their fear as best they could.

The plane was in the air and there was no turning back. I thought the army would not let a few hundred guys jump if there were any true danger.

Again, strength in numbers was my main thought.

There are two lights at each side door of the plane. One is red and one is green. When we get near the drop zone the red light comes on. This is the signal to get ready.

At this point the doors are opened on both sides of the plane. Then the Sgt. in charge starts yelling the jump commands.

The first command is "Get Ready". The next command is "Stand Up". Now the sweat is flowing steadily. Here we go; all thoughts are "we". I'm not doing this alone.

Next is "Hook Up", which is where our static line connects our parachute to the cable running from the back to the front of the plane. The next commands have us checking our equipment and also the equipment of the person directly in front of us.

We are getting close and I am very nervous, however, there is no turning back.

My brother should rot in hell.

Then the next command is yelled out, "Stand in the Door". This is where the first person stands in the door of the plane with their toes hanging over the edge of the door and both hands holding on to the side of the open door waiting for the green light and the last command.

The green light turns and the Sgt. yells out the last command, "Go". The man in the door jumps. The next man stands in the door, the Sgt. again yells "Go" and he jumps. We are shuffling closer to the door so there is no stopping the line now.

As I get closer to the door I can see out. We are definitely in the air and the ground looks far away. "What am I doing here?" It now becomes my turn.

I shuffle to the door and stand in it for a second. The Sgt. yells "Go" and I jump into the air.

I was to count four seconds and then look up. If I didn't see my canopy open, I was to pull the D-ring on my reserve. I didn't remember to count, I just looked up and there was the most beautiful sight I ever saw in my life. My canopy was wide open and I was floating gently to the earth.

WOW! This was really cool. Not only did I overcome my biggest fear, but also I am floating in the air by myself. I am now officially a paratrooper. No one could ever take that away from me.

As I descended down I began to realize how cool this really was. The only sound was the wind whooshing around me.

I began to relax and all my fear was completely gone. I bent my knees like I was taught. I folded my arms over my reserve and just looked all around. It was beautiful.

My brother was right. This was something I will never forget. He was always right. I have to remember to thank him.

As I neared the ground I remembered my instructions, relax, bend your knees, and do the PLF. I got closer and closer to the ground. The instructions were going through my head.

I was completely relaxed and ready to land. Just before my landing I prepared for my PLF.

I hit the ground and the first thing that hit the ground was the bottom of my toes like instructed. Then the next thing that hit was my buttock. It seemed I relaxed a little too much.

It hurt at first and I stayed on the ground for a moment. A Sgt. and his driver pulled up to me in a jeep and asked if I was hurt. My first thought was "a ride back" so I said "yes, I think I hurt my leg."

The Sgt. told me to get up shake it off and double time back to our group area, which was on the other side of the drop zone. I lost my free ride, but nevertheless I did it. I jumped out of an airplane.

What a rush!

The next two days consisted of three more jumps. All went well and I didn't get hurt from landing. I really looked forward to our next jumps.

Thursday was the last jump. This jump was going to be different.

It was a combat jump. This means we carry our web gear and also a rifle. It seemed like it was going to be okay, but I was leery of different.

When we arrived at the hanger we received our parachutes along with our other equipment. Everything seemed normal.

Then we were told that the rifle pack which is a canvas bag that we placed our rifle into had two straps. The upper strap tied to our web gear, the lower strap tied around our leg.

The thing to remember was that after you jump out of the plane you must un-tie the lower strap because if you don't it could break your leg when you land. We loaded into the plane like before and took off for our final jump in jump school.

"Go" and off I went for my final jump. Like before, everything was picture perfect; I really liked this jumping thing. Again, I relaxed, not too much, and enjoyed the view.

By this time I knew what to expect. I felt very comfortable and enjoyed the peaceful descent. I looked all around and soaked in the view from about 1,200 feet above the ground.

Then I heard something, like someone yelling. I looked around and saw nothing; I had no idea what it was.

It started getting louder so I looked down at the ground. I saw a Sgt. with a bullhorn yelling something up at me but I couldn't make it out.

As I descended, I leaned down as much as I could to hear. I finally was able to make out what he was saying; "Untie your leg strap".

I forgot to untie the lower strap around my leg. I reached down and pulled the leg strap just as I hit the ground.

This time I was hurt, the impact was not pretty. I hit my feet, then my buttock, and then my head. I thought for sure something was broken.

Again, a Sgt. and his driver pulled up and asked if I was hurt. This time I was serious when I said, "Yes, I think I might have broken something". He looked at me and said, "Shake it off and double time back to the group".

I slowly got up, brushed myself off and ran back, everything was fine. When I arrived at the group area, everyone was hollering and congratulating each other.

It was then that I realized what I had done. I felt great, like I could do anything.

When we graduated on Friday we were given our "Wings", signifying that we were now "Airborne" and were given our orders.

I wanted to go to the 82nd Airborne because that is the only unit I really ever heard of. But instead I was going to the 101st Airborne, someplace in Kentucky.

101st AIRBORNE

Ft. Campbell, Kentucky, home of the 101st Airborne Division.

The Airborne started at Ft. Benning, Georgia in 1940 with a parachute platoon commanded by Major Bob Sink. The Germans had shown the advantages of airborne units and we knew we had to do the same.

The most significant moment in the history of the 101st Airborne Division occurred during WWII.

The 101st Airborne Division fought their way into the city of Bastogne, Belgium.

Several German panzer units surrounded them in the besieged city. The German commander sent a messenger to General Mc Aullif demanding he surrender. The General sent back his reply, "Nuts".

They held on until help arrived and continued to play a major role in the victory over Germany. The "Airborne" rapidly became one of the 'elite' forces in the army.

"Why would anyone want to jump out of a perfectly good airplane?" I have been asked that question many times in my life. Usually I just laugh and make some kind of joke about it.

The truth is that when you go "Airborne" you are looked upon by regular units as someone special. We wear jump boots with our pants legs tucked in instead of shoes.

We wear a cap with a parachute logo on the front instead of hat with a brim.

But the most significant difference between the "Airborne" and "Legs" (non-airborne) is we wear "Jump Wings" on our chest. The wings signify who we are and what we do.

Our job is to do what regular units cannot do. Jump in behind enemy lines. We train harder and longer. We are the first army units to go into action. Special Forces, UDT's, Seals, and any other special operations units must first become "Airborne."

Paratroopers are respected everywhere they go. We do everything all other units do; only we get there faster, much faster.

Aviation Battalion

My orders were to report to the Aviation Battalion. I had no idea what to expect. Why the aviation battalion?

When I arrived I was taken to a modern building which was my new barracks. No more wooden buildings left over from WWI. This was really nice.

There were only two people assigned to a room. Everything about the aviation battalion was top notch, only what was I doing here?

The reason I was sent to the aviation battalion was to train to become a "Pathfinder", whatever that was. In the next few days of classes I learned what a "Pathfinder" does.

A "Pathfinder" is lowered by helicopter or jumps into an area with a rifle and a chainsaw. Once on the ground he is to clear enough brush in order for a helicopter to land.

The helicopter will bring more men with rifles and chainsaws to clear a larger area. With the larger area cleared, more helicopters carrying engineers and heavy equipment are brought in to clear a very large area and start construction of an airstrip.

This sounded good. No twenty-mile hikes. No bivouacs. Light duty, and best of all, only two people to a room, not twenty or thirty.

Every day we started with PT which wasn't bad at all. After PT we went to mess for as long as we wanted. No short time limit like before. Then we played games like dodge ball, baseball, & football.

This was not what I expected. This was too good to be true.

Cherry Jump

When you complete jump school and are assigned to a regular unit, your first jump is called your "Cherry Jump". Well it *was* time for my cherry jump. I had no idea what was in store for me.

We were too small a unit to warrant a jump by ourselves, so we would attach ourselves to another unit, usually infantry, and jump with them. Since we were already at the airbase at Ft. Campbell we didn't have far to go.

The fear of jumping was completely gone. I was looking forward to it. We loaded onto the plane. No waiting on the airstrip like jump school.

Once in the plane, we sat and the plane taxied and then took off. I was having a good time. Everyone was talking as if they were back in the barracks. No praying. No sweating. No nervousness. It was great and I loved it.

Then the red light went on and the command to get ready was issued. We went through the jump commands just like in school with no problem. After about ten minutes and about 1200 feet, the red light turned off and the green light came on. Everyone started shuffling to the door. I was getting closer and closer.

When it was my turn to stand in the door, the guy behind me yelled loud and clear "Talerico, here's your chute" as he handed me my parachute.

As I left the airplane, holding my parachute, my life flashed in front of me. I was going to die right here and right now.

He must have unhooked the clip from the cable in the plane. That was his job, to make sure I was hooked up, that is how we did it in training.

Now I am going to die, just like I dreamt as a child. I'm going to fall and this time I'm not going to wake up. I started to pray, hard and fast, I didn't have much time so I tried to get as many prayers in as possible before I smacked into the ground. "Our Father", "Hail Mary", over and over, I prayed more than any other time in my life. I am going to die. This is it.

I have so many people to say goodbye to, except my brother, Bill, this was all his idea, "Go Airborne", I hate him with a passion. He should be falling instead of me. He should die like this.

Knowing him, he is probably at a frat party having a great time while I die. This was it. Goodbye world.

Then I felt a familiar tug. I looked up and there was my canopy wide open as I was falling gracefully to the ground. This was a trick that was pulled on most guys making their cherry jump.

The guy behind me had hooked me up. He then proceeded to pull about five feet of my parachute out of its pack. This would not affect the proper functioning of the parachute; however, it had a tremendous effect on the unknowing person wearing the chute.

Welcome to the "Airborne". I just made my cherry jump.

One month later I was transferred to an infantry battalion.

501st INFANTRY

"B" Company

I arrived at "B" company early October. I didn't realize how cold Kentucky got during the winter. It was as cold, if not colder, than New Jersey.

Now I am in the infantry. A ground pounder, grunt, dogface, and all the other names associated with the worst job in the military.

No more semi-private rooms. No more dodge ball and other games during the day. Mess was with 200 guys at a time. Not 20 like in the aviation battalion.

I knew immediately I didn't like this.

Abraham

When I arrived at "B" company, I was sent upstairs to the 3rd
platoon. When I walked into the platoon area I felt like I was back
in basic. Along both sides of the room were cubicles. Each
cubicle had two beds, two wall lockers and two footlockers.

The fire team leader I was assigned to looked around and said
there were no available bunks, so I should take Pvt. Lowman
Abraham's bunk until he returns from leave.

I didn't think anything of it and threw my duffle bag on the bunk. I
couldn't use the wall or footlocker because they weren't mine, plus
they were locked. So I just placed my clothes on top of the
footlocker.

Someone asked me what I was doing. I said I was waiting for my
own bunk and was told to use Abraham's bunk until then. He told
me that I shouldn't be using Abraham's bunk because Abraham
wouldn't like it.

I just shrugged it off. Another guy came over and said pretty much
the same thing as the first guy. Who the hell is this Abraham,
anyway?

I might just have to kick his ass when he returns. After all I was a
Jersey boy and no one pushes us around. If this guy Abraham
starts anything, I will end it nice and quick.

I had absolutely no fear of this Abraham.

After a few days, I was lying on my (Abraham's) bunk reading a
magazine. It was late afternoon and everybody was kicking back
waiting for the mess hall to open up. All of a sudden I hear this
loud bellowing, "WHAT THE FUCK! WHO THE FUCK IS IN MY
BUNK?"

I jumped up and was face to face with the biggest, meanest
looking, black guy I ever saw in my life. His eyes were red and

filled with hate, and I was in his bunk.

Suddenly, my attitude made a complete change. Being a Jersey boy meant nothing. My thoughts of "kick his ass" went to "help".

He started taking my clothes off "his" footlocker and threw them in the middle of the barracks floor. I looked around for anything that belonged to me. I saw some of my clothes at the side of his bed and grabbed them and threw them on the floor. My boots also went flying across the barracks along with anything of mine I could find.

I started cursing and saying things like "I told them I shouldn't take your fucking bunk. They made me do it." He didn't know what to think. After a very short while I stopped, looked around for anything I missed and walked to the middle of the room to pick up my stuff. Abraham began to calm down once all my stuff was out of his area.

Over the next six months or so, Abraham would tell us how bad he was, and how he was going to destroy "Charlie" (Viet Cong) single-handed. He didn't need us. We would only get in his way.

He couldn't wait to get to Vietnam. Every day we heard the same thing, over and over. He carried a knife on his belt and another one tied to his leg.

He would tell us how he was going to cut their throats. Cut off their heads and shit down their necks.

When he said these things we all acknowledged it with cheers and approval. We didn't dare disagree with him. Behind his back we all thought the same thing. He will probably be the first person to run.

We couldn't wait to hear the next tirade of bullshit coming from Abraham. All talk, was putting it nicely. He was almost embarrassing.

We didn't know back at Ft. Campbell, but Abraham would have his chance.

Capt. Paul C. Clark

Our company commander was Capt. Paul C. Clark; he was about six foot four and about 200 pounds, and kind of lanky.

We didn't have much contact with him and that was good. The few times he would address us he had to be prompted by the 1st Sgt., who never left his side.

The only time we spoke to Capt. Clark was payday when he gave us our pay, and then it wasn't more than our name, a quick glance, and "Next".

The word around the barracks was that Capt. Clark was formerly a cook. He went to OCS and became an officer.

We didn't think much about him. We hardly ever saw him. He probably was a bad cook anyway.

1st. Sgt. Bobby R. Poe

1st Sgt. Bobby R. Poe was "B" company's 1st Sgt. and right hand man to Capt. Clark. Capt. Clark never went anywhere without Sgt. Poe.

1st. Sgt. Poe joined the army at the age of fifteen. By the time he reached twenty-five he had made 1st. Sgt.

He had a terrible disposition; he didn't like anyone, never smiled, and was always yelling about something. Like Capt. Clark, we didn't have much contact with Sgt. Poe either and that too was a good thing.

Lt. J. Michael Deems

Second Lt. J. Michael Deems was my platoon leader. He was the person who we took orders from.

He must have been twenty-two or twenty-three, blonde hair and a fair face. He was about my size and he was in good shape.

The thing I remember the most was his personality. He was not like the other officers I met.

He was the first "true" leader. Someone we felt comfortable talking to. We could ask him anything and he would answer without making us feel like idiots.

Everyone in our platoon looked up to Lt. Deems. He was one of us.

I heard he graduated from West Point, which probably made him the smartest officer in the company.

When we had any kind of inspection, he and the platoon Sgt. would check us and if something was wrong Lt. Deems would simply point out the problem, tell us to fix it and then he would move on to the next guy.

Lt. Deems was the one officer that anyone would want as his or her leader in wartime.

Sgt. Corbett

Sgt. J. D. Corbett was our platoon Sgt. He was the enforcer of Lt. Deems orders. Sgt. Corbett was about six feet two, black, and about 200 pounds. He also had a pencil thin mustache.

He was a "lifer" and loved the army life. Sgt. Corbett was a tough but fair Sgt. He would tell us what we had to do and help us when we needed it. For a "lifer", Sgt. Corbett was an intelligent person.

He knew the army and everything about the infantry. He would carry on occasionally with the other "lifer" Sgts. He was also laid back and didn't give anyone any unnecessary hassle.

He was probably this way because of Lt. Deems. The two of them worked together, not against each other like some of the other platoons.

RTO

One day Sgt. Corbett asked if anyone would like to volunteer to become a radio operator. I didn't know anything about radios but I thought this would help to get me promoted, so I volunteered. I was given a PRC 25 radio to learn.

A PRC 25 radio, or better known as a "prick 25" is about 14 inches across, 18 inches down, about 4 inches thick and weighs 24.7 pounds. This would replace the M60 machine gun ammo I would normally carry.

I didn't know much about the internal workings of the radio, except it had an 8-foot antennae and it went under my rut sack (backpack). I liked the fact that I would be the platoon RTO (Radio Telephone Operator), and would be working directly for Lt. Deems.

This is a job that I liked and I tried to do my best. I was always prepared. Well, most times. Lt. Deems liked the job I was doing.

I had a good job. I made some good friends, and I was on my way.

Pvt. Steve Becsei

Steve Becsei arrived at "B" Company around the same time as me. He was assigned to my squad and we hit it off right away. He was from South Bend, Indiana and was a die-hard Notre Dame fan.

He was about 5' 10" and around 160 pounds, but he had an attitude and a mouth that would make you think he was 6' 4" and 220 pounds if you didn't know any better.

I got a kick out of his mouthing off about different things. We used to rank each other to pass the time and he was a pro at it. Things like "Your mama's so fat, etc., etc." He would get going and go on for hours. He had absolutely no fear, especially after a few drinks.

One time, Becsei and I were in Hopkinsville at a diner. It was around midnight when four marines walked in. They were in fatigue uniforms and were minding their own business. From the looks of them, they were all in excellent shape and sober.

When Steve saw them he looked at them and laughed. While laughing he said "Hey, look at the jarheads, they don't have any necks." They came back with some remark and that started Steve going. He rambled on about how the marines were nothing and the odds were even, four of them and two of us.

I placed my head in my hands and figured he was going to start something and I was going to get my ass kicked. I kept telling him to shut up but he kept going. Then one of the marines made a challenge and Becsei jumped to his feet and said, "If you feel froggy, jump." The four marines stared at him for a few seconds, then turned and walked away. Becsei kept on mouthing off as they walked out of the diner. I told him he was crazy for starting trouble but then he started ranking on me. I just ignored him and we left the diner.

Pvt. Roger Bray

Roger Bray, or "Ski" as he was known, also arrived around November of 1965. He was assigned to the weapons platoon.

Roger was from South River New Jersey, a Jersey boy. We became friends right away.

He was about 5' 11" and 180 pounds, and had a quiet disposition, which was a welcome relief compared to the constant ramblings of Becsei.

The 11th General Order

The army has this thing called the general orders. During my career there were 10 general orders having to do with following military rule, standing guard, etc. When asked what the 11th general order is, the correct response is "To remember the first 10 orders".

One December day, while in our morning formation, waiting for Capt. Clark and Sgt. Poe to give us our morning briefing, Sgt. Corbett walked up to Pvt. Spence.

Robert Spence was a skinny, somewhat of a wiseass hillbilly type. He was a funny guy who always made us laugh. He wasn't very big, and compared to Sgt. Corbett he was tiny.

Standing directly in front of Spence, Sgt. Corbett, in a relatively loud voice looked down at Pvt. Spence and said "Pvt. Spence, what is the 11th general order"?

Pvt. Spence with absolutely no hesitation said in a similarly loud voice, "Sgt. the 11th general order is Thou shalt not cultivate around thine lip what grows wild around thine ass."

We all stood in shock. Sgt. Corbett had never been tested or ridiculed by anyone and we were waiting for his anger to befall on Spence.

Sgt. Corbett stood with a surprised look on his face for what seemed like an eternity. But then, all of a sudden he cracked up laughing. While laughing he just walked away. This was Sgt. Corbett, a military guy through and through, but he was one of us.

Christmas 1965

One mid December morning, during our company formation, the bottom dropped out of my military career. While barking out the orders for the day, Sgt. Poe, in a loud and clear voice yelled out, "Oh, and when the formation is over, Pvt. Talerico is to report to the company commander's office. It seems that his Mommy wants him home for Christmas."

What? What is going on? Everyone in my platoon turned and looked at me. I felt like my world just collapsed. How humiliating. What is happening?

All Christmas leaves had been cancelled due to pending orders for Vietnam. I, like everyone else scheduled for Christmas leave, notified my parents that I would not be coming home. I never expected, wanted, or imagined anything like this happening.

I went to see Capt. Clark as ordered and he informed me that all leaves were cancelled and I was to inform my family of that. I did just that as soon as I left his office.

I called home and was told by both my mother and my father that no such request had been made by them. I felt that they were not telling me the truth because of my mother's brother Bobby, who was killed in WWII.

They never spoke much of my uncle Bobby. But as a young boy I would sneak into my Mother's cedar chest which contained old letters, photos, and a recording my uncle made while in England, preparing for the invasion of Normandy.

I would play the record and listen to him talk to my mother and then sing to her. It always made me cry, but I was fascinated by it. I still listen to his voice today.

I was angry and let them know that what happened was the most embarrassing thing that has happened to me in the army. They assured me that they had nothing to do with it and that it wouldn't happen again.

Sgt. Poe then informed me that I was to report to KP (Kitchen Patrol) the next morning. This was the first time I had KP. I was to become an expert at peeling potatoes in a very short time. I didn't go on leave for Christmas, but now I was on Sgt. Poe's shit list, and that was not a good place to be.

Shain's Cherry Jump

Danny Shain was a big, strong, farm boy from somewhere In the mid-west. When he arrived he was assigned to my platoon and we immediately became friends. He was a likable guy who was always up for whatever anyone wanted to do.

One day someone brought in a couple of pairs of boxing gloves. I thought I was a pretty good fighter so I went up against Shain. He quickly let me know that I was not a pretty good fighter like I thought, but rather a pretty good punching bag for him. My boxing career in the army lasted about 20 seconds. After that I was happy being a spectator.

We were notified that our company was going to make a jump. This was a practice jump we made every few weeks, or so. It was also going to be Pvt. Shain's cherry jump. What else could I do? I made sure I was behind Shain as we got into the plane and was all set to properly indoctrinate him into the airborne, and revenge for the whipping he gave me while boxing.

The jump commands began; we all stood up, hooked up, etc. and got ready to jump. While waiting for the green light, I started pulling some of Shain's parachute out of his pack.

I pulled about five feet of chute and was holding on to it. When the green light went on we started shuffling to the door. When Shain made it to the door I handed him his chute just as the Sgt. said, "Go".

Now Danny Shain was one of the biggest and strongest guys in our platoon. When we would go out to Hopkinsville, Clarksville, or even to one of the enlisted men's clubs on the base, we liked having Danny Shain with us. He was our bodyguard. His presence alone would scare people away.

Well, he let out a scream that would rank up there with any Hollywood horror film scream. It was perfect and I loved it. I was next and made another great jump. I felt really cool on the way down. I got Shain back. I was king of the hill.

When I landed, I began gathering up my parachute. I was in no hurry until all of a sudden I see Danny Shain, running at top speed towards me screaming something. I couldn't make out the words exactly, but I remember words like "I'm going to kill you", and "You're going to die", and other similar words.

I started running toward the group area. I figured I could outlast him, and with my life on the line, I was sure I could. After a while he started to tire and slow down. When he finally stopped, I cautiously walked over to him and with a big smile said, "Welcome to the airborne." We were friends and I knew once he got over the initial shock he would be fine. He looked up at me and I knew he really wanted to hit me, but he was just too tired. We walked back and agreed to welcome the next guy together.

Riggers

One of my biggest concerns about jumping out of an airplane was
that I might have to pack my own chute. When I found out that
other people packed them I felt a lot better.

The people who pack all the parachutes are called "riggers."
Riggers would pack chutes all day. They would throw their packed
chutes into a bin reserved just for them.

Every once in a while a Sgt. would pick a chute out of a riggers
bin and he would have to make a jump using that chute. This way
they were more careful.

I only toured the riggers area one time, but that was enough.
While watching one rigger pack a chute, I noticed he was cutting
suspension lines and risers and then replacing them.

He would discard the cut items into a barrel next to his bin. I kept
watching him work, asking questions about how the chute actually
functions, and watching him throw away worn or torn parts.

He would discard the cut items into a barrel next to his bin. I kept
watching him work, asking questions about how the chute actually
functions, and watching him throw away worn or torn parts.

A rigger was checking a chute's static line. This is the eight-foot
cord that connects to the cable in the plane and pulls the chute
out when you jump. He cut the cord at the chute and threw it in
the bin.

I asked him what was going to happen to all these worn parts and
he said they were garbage. I asked if I could keep the static line
he just threw away as a souvenir and he said sure. Souvenir, my
ass. This was going to be used for the next cherry jumper.

We're going to kick it up a notch.

The River Crossing

We sat in stands at the edge of a small river and we were all shivering from the cold. It was about 30 feet across and moving steadily but not too fast.

We were to learn how to cross a river or creek, army style. The instructor, a Sgt, told us that one person must strip down to his shorts, tie a rope around his waist, jump into the river and swim to the other side and tie his end to a tree. Then another person must tie the other end of the rope to a tree on this side of the river.

Another Sgt. started stripping down to his shorts while we watched in fear. We knew what was coming. He tied the rope around his waist and then jumped into the river and swam to the other side. After tying his end to a tree, another Sgt. tied our end to a tree and made sure the rope was taught.

Then the Sgt. on our side, while fully clothed, held onto the rope and got into the water. When he did this, the rope started stretching. Hand over hand he eventually made it to the other side. The rope was never less than a foot above the water.

The instructor told us that there should never be more than one man on the rope because it would stretch the rope too much and cause it to go below the water level.

Then he told us to line up and get ready to cross the river. The thought of going in that icy water was unthinkable and everyone started moaning and complaining. The Sgts started laughing and told us that they were just kidding and we didn't have to go in the water.

There is a God.

The First Phone Call

Around February 1966, I was called down to the company commander's office. I had no idea what the problem was. I hadn't any details for a few weeks and everything seemed to quiet down as far as Sgt. Poe and I were concerned. I was doing a good job learning the radio and everything was running smoothly.

When I reported to Sgt. Poe, he informed me that I was to be transferred to Fort Monmouth, NJ.

Fort Monmouth, NJ is about one hour from my hometown of Little Falls, NJ. it is also near Monmouth College and Monmouth racetrack where I would go with my father once in a while. But the best part about Ft. Monmouth is that it is on the ocean.

I was to report to the signal battalion and remain there for the duration of my two years in the army.

I should have signed the papers, transferred to Ft. Monmouth, and spent the rest of my tour of duty in comfort and safety. That is what 99.9% of my unit would have done if given the chance, but not me.

I spent eight weeks of AIT and 3 weeks of jump school to get here. I accomplished my goal of jumping out of an airplane.

Now I'm supposed to give it all up and become a "leg"? No way! "Legs" were nothing, dirt, pond scum, and the bottom of the barrel. The only thing lower than an army leg is a marine leg.

I asked Sgt. Poe why I had to sign the orders. Usually the army just gives you the orders and you follow them. He said, "A congressman called the CO (commanding officer) and asked him to transfer you, so just sign the papers."

I asked him if it was a request on my part to be transferred and he said yes. That's all I needed to know.

I refused to sign the papers and explained to Sgt. Poe that I wanted to stay with the unit and go to Vietnam. It wasn't that I wanted to go to war and kill people. I had absolutely no desire for either. I just wanted to stay with the 101st Airborne.

I had been brainwashed for months about the airborne and how they were so much better than the regular army. I also had several friends and the thought of them going off to Vietnam and me staying behind because of political influence was unthinkable.

I would never be able to live with myself.

Refusing to sign the transfer papers was not the smartest thing I ever did. Every day I had the worst details, and of course every other day I had KP.

By this time I knew all the cooks. I could peel a potato in less than 10 seconds. There wasn't much left to it by then, but I was fast. Pots and pans were a piece of cake for me. I figure I peeled about 10,000 potatoes and washed about 200 pots and pans.

I never understood why my company commander and 1st Sgt. were angry. I wanted to stay with the unit. I was doing a good job with no problems, and I got along with everyone.

I thought they would be happy to have someone who actually wanted to be there. But, the important thing was that I was still a member of the 101st Airborne.

When I called home I was told that they knew nothing about it. I remember yelling at my mother telling her about all the trouble I was in because of the phone call. She assured me that they had no idea who was doing it.

The "Ham Stretcher"

I was given KP every other day because I would not sign my transfer papers. When you get KP duty you must report to the mess hall around 5:00 AM to help prepare for the morning breakfast.

This particular morning there was a different cook in charge. We were ahead of schedule for breakfast and I was even working on the lunch potatoes. The cook was in a good mood and decided to play a joke on me.

He called over to me and said, "Talerico, go to "A" company and get their "ham stretcher". We don't have enough ham for lunch".

Now I have been on KP what seemed like forever. I heard all the jokes and stories, even the ham stretcher story. There is no such thing as a ham stretcher. It is designed to make you look like a fool when you go around asking for one.

I immediately left the mess hall and went to "A" company's mess hall. I went up to the cook in charge and said, "B Company doesn't have enough ham for lunch and would like to borrow your ham stretcher."

The cook laughed a bit and said he would look for it.' I knew what was next. He came back and said it was loaned to "C" Company.

This is what I knew he would say, but I had to go to the first place I was told. I took off and went back to my platoon area where everyone was sitting around taking it easy. I stayed there until 5:00 pm the end of my shift.

When I returned the cook asked me where I was all day and I told him I went to A company like he ordered me to, they sent me to C Company. They sent me to HQ Company, etc., all over the base.

He looked at me knowing damn well I was lying through my teeth,

but it was his joke. I just lucked out and knew about it ahead of time. This was one KP that wasn't bad.
Meyer's Cherry Jump

We received a new person in our platoon. His name was Duane Meyer. He was about six feet and weighed about one hundred eighty pounds.

He seemed like a nice guy and we immediately became friends, but the best thing about Duane Meyer was this was his first regular unit. Therefore he was going to make his "cherry jump" with us.

Preparations were made. Danny Shain was informed about Meyer's cherry jump and instructed to get behind me when we loaded the plane. The very next jump we were ready, we had everything planned down to Meyer's exit from the plane.

I brought the extra static line I had gotten from the rigger and was anxious to see the look on Meyer's face when I handed him the clip.

We boarded the plane as planned. Meyer was to jump about 15th in line. I was 16th, and Shain was 17th. The plane took off and was nearing the drop zone.

The red light went on and we stood up and went through the jump commands, including the command where I check the person in front of me.

I made sure he was hooked up properly. I didn't even have the spare static line out of my pocket yet. I didn't want to make any mistakes and hook up the spare.

Making sure he was set and ready to go, I took out the spare static line and held it by the hook that gets clipped inside the plane. I showed the clip to Shain and he laughed in approval.

Now it's okay to scare someone else. We got the go light and began our shuffle. I yelled to Meyer asking him if he was all right. He said he was. That would change.

We shuffled closer to the door and it was Meyer's turn to stand in the door. As soon as he got in the door I yelled at him while handing him the clip to the spare static line, I yelled. "Meyer, I forgot to hook you up."

He turned and looked right into my eyes. His eyes and mouth were wide open and he looked like he was going to die. There was no screaming, it was beyond that. The look on his face was one of complete horror. And then he was gone.

I was next and made my jump. When I landed I completely expected to see him running after me like Shain did.

This time when I looked to see where Meyer was, I saw him with his chute wrapped up like normal and he was walking towards me.

When he approached me I said "Welcome to the airborne, you just made your cherry jump." The only thing he cared about was if he could keep the spare static line.

By this time Shain had joined us and was wondering why he wasn't angry. Meyer said it scared the daylights out of him but it was great. I looked at Shain and said, "See, not everyone is a pussy".

He started after me again, and again I outran him.

What a group! Roger Bray was the more down to Earth type, sensible and firm.

Steve Becsei was the more vocal one of the group and usually the one who suggested the things we should do.

Duane Meyer was the quiet one who went along with everything.

Danny Shain was the big one of the group but didn't stand a chance against Becsei's ramblings.

Marine Maneuvers

For a training exercise, we were going to go up against the marines stationed at Camp LeJeune, NC. Up to this point I hadn't had much respect for marines. The way I figured, they were better than legs, everyone was better than legs, but they were nothing compared to the airborne.

Marines were gung ho and brainwashed to the point where they did the best job possible, win at all cost, and willing to die for the (corps) Quitting was something a marine would never do, no matter what the consequences.

The plan was to jump into Camp LeJeune and have war maneuvers against the marines. This was going to be a test of their best against the army's best. We thought it was going to be difficult because they were marines and stupid enough to try really hard to win.

We had the advantage of having approximately 1,000 paratroopers jump into their territory. The sight of 1,000 paratroopers is awesome. Some say it looks like 10,000. It's a sight that would scare the living daylights out of anyone.

When it came time for our jump everything went smoothly. One guy's static line didn't break off at his chute and he was dragging alongside the airplane. He was finally cut off over the town. That must have been a sight for the townsfolk to see an invasion of one. He was okay and returned to his unit.

After landing and rendezvousing with our units, we started our patrols. We walked most of the first day. Just before dusk we dug foxholes and set up for the night. No contact with the marines. Chow time came and hot food was trucked out to us.

We had c-rations during the day, but at night we had nice hot food. We took turns standing guard. We stood guard from 6:00

pm until 6:00 am. There were four people to a foxhole (position). Each person stood guard for three hours and then woke up the next person. This wasn't bad at all. Since we were emulating combat conditions, there were no fires.

The second day we started our patrols as usual, only this time we ran into a few marines. They were easy to spot and we surrounded them. When we approached, they immediately held their arms up and surrendered. What a bunch of candy-asses these marines were. We brought them back and held them as POWs. By the end of the day we had captured about ten marines with no problem.

Marines were nothing like we had grown up to believe. They were too eager to surrender. How they were so heroic in WWII was beyond us. We were almost embarrassed at how easy it was to win each confrontation. I lost what little respect I had for the marine corp and was beginning to realize our mighty airborne was as good as we were told.

The airborne was superior to any other fighting unit. We were the elite of the combat units in all the services. Again, at the end of the day we had our meals brought in. We even fed the marines. After all, these were only maneuvers.

The third day was even more surprising than the first two days. We captured about 20 more marines with no resistance. We were feeling good about ourselves.

When we brought them back to our base we placed them in our jail area (a separate area where they were to stay). When they saw the other marines they asked, "Is it true?" the marines already captured the previous day said, "Yes, they have hot meals at night, and there's plenty of it".

They were not afraid of us, they were not candy-asses, and they were not stupid. They just wanted something hot to eat and we had it. Not really giving a damn about the maneuvers, they were looking for what we had; hot food. Our egos were deflated, and my respect for marines went right back up there with the airborne.

The Second Phone Call

While polishing my boots in the barracks one afternoon, a clerk in the CO's office told me to report to the CO. It seemed another congressman had him on the phone.

I literally ran downstairs hoping to catch this guy on the phone and tell him to leave me alone. By the time I got there he had already hung up. His message was clear, "Why haven't I been transferred to Ft. Monmouth?"

Sgt. Poe, again with the transfer papers in front of him on the desk, told me to sign the papers. Again I refused, giving the same reason as before. He informed me that they were going to step up my details until I sign the papers. I was on KP every other day and in between I had every other detail. If it was a crummy job, I got it. What else could he possibly do?

At this point it wasn't staying airborne that I wanted, I just didn't want to give in to their pressure. I hated Poe and Clark. I had no respect for either of them, but I wanted to stay with them. What a moron I was. If I had any brains, I would have packed my bags and hopped on the next plane out of there.

Again, no one at home had any idea what was going on, but of course I knew better.

12-Week Training Cycle

We started our ATT (Army Training Test). This was to be a 12-week training cycle. We would jump out Sunday night, spend the week in the field and then be brought back by truck on Friday, usually at night.

We would have an equipment inspection Saturday morning, then another inspection Sunday afternoon.

There were graders (soldiers attached to each unit and each area of the unit who were grading us on every detail of our operation) all over the place making notes about everything. I was our platoon's RTO and assigned to our platoon leader, Lt. Deems. All I had to do was keep my radio working and follow Lt. Deems wherever he went.

First Helicopter Ride

I had never been in a helicopter before so when I heard we were going to train on them it sounded like fun. We were told that we were going on the same helicopters used in Vietnam so we needed to get used to them. We didn't have to bring anything other than our web gear. We're just going for a ride.

The helicopters had an opening about five feet wide directly behind the pilot and co-pilot. Hanging halfway outside the helicopter was a machine gunner. Further back was a single seat exposed to the outside.

About five helicopters arrived and we were already in groups of about ten. When we were told to get in the helicopters I noticed the single seat next to the gunner. I went for that particular seat because I thought it would be cool to sit on the edge of the helicopter rather than be grouped in the main section with the others.

I climbed into the seat. The gunner told me to fasten my seat belt. It was a strap that went across my waist, no problem. Then he told me to close the door. I grabbed hold of the door and closed it like he said.

It was dark out when we finally took off. It was as I expected. We went about 500 feet in the air and I could see clearly all around even though it was at night. We flew for about 20 minutes then returned to get the next group of soldiers. I liked helicopters a lot and I was always going to get the side seat if I could.

Jamache Club

One Saturday night a few of us decided to go drinking at the Jamache club, a local enlisted men's club on the base. We spent the week in the freezing cold and were going back on Sunday, so why not?

We got to the club and started drinking kamikazes and zombies. I didn't know what they were, but what the hell, why not. We all drank them and after a while all of us, except Danny Shain, were on the floor.

From what I was told, Shain called for a cab and carried us, one at a time, into the cab. We were taken back to our barracks and Shain again carried us into the barracks. I don't remember anything other than someone saying, "Hey, Talerico, here's your drink."

The Inspection

The next day, Sunday, we were to have our usual inspection around 1:00 pm. At about 12:50, Becsei woke me up and told me to get ready for inspection. Apparently I passed out and was asleep all night and all day. When he woke me up I was a mess. I still had my fatigues on from the night before and I smelled and looked really bad.

Someone yelled "Attention" signifying Lt. Deems and Sgt. Corbett were in the room and inspection was to start. Everyone stood by their footlockers and was ready, except me. I struggled to just stand up, let alone at attention.

I grabbed my rifle and threw it over my right shoulder. Then I grabbed my web gear and threw it over my left shoulder. My shirt was sweaty and unbuttoned, and I was unshaven, smelly, and looked like something the cat dragged in.

As Lt Deems walked down my side of the room he would point out infractions, like a belt buckle not shiny enough, or maybe a shirt not tucked in properly, but nothing serious. I didn't care about anything other than going back to sleep.

When Lt Deems and Sgt. Corbett walked in front of me I was leaning on the cubicle wall. Sgt. Corbett took one look at me, his eyes wide open like he was in shock. Lt. Deems took one look at me and asked, "Rough night?" to which I said, "Yes sir". He then asked, "Are you going to be ready for tonight's jump?" to which I replied, "Yes sir". He acknowledged my reply and moved on to the next guy and never brought the incident up again.

My only reasoning for his reaction was that he was well aware of the treatment I was getting from Capt. Clark and Sgt. Poe, maybe he thought I deserved a break, or maybe the punishment for such an infraction of the rules would be more severe than he was willing to give out. I'll never know for sure.

That night I was ready and was looking good, except I felt like I was going to die.

Larry Knight

Larry Knight was in my company He was well liked by everyone who knew him. He didn't hang around with my group of friends. Nevertheless he got along with everyone.

As part of the ATT's we were to have a live fire exercise. We were going to go to Horseshoe Mountain and fire live ammunition. When we arrived at Horseshoe Mountain we immediately realized how it got its name. The mountain was more of a ridge, but it was in the shape of a horseshoe. From one tip of the horseshoe to the other tip of the horseshoe was about a hundred yards across.

In between the two tips and most of the rest of the area we were to fire in was nothing but some weeds and a sprinkling of shrubs, except for one small area. This area had some taller shrubs, a tree, and a ditch. The entire area was no more than a small backyard, an oasis.

That was it. There were no other targets for us to aim at other than the tree and surrounding area. Our entire company was on the ridge waiting for orders to open fire.

The CO. Capt. Clark gave the order to open fire and our entire company of almost 200 guys open fired on the oasis.

We each emptied at least one magazine of 20 rounds; some reloaded and emptied another magazine. I, along with most of the others aimed at the tree. There were no other real targets. Then all hell broke loose.

All of a sudden the order to cease-fire was given. Not in the usual manner, but in a panic.

Two soldiers had been sent to the oasis as LP's (Listening Posts) but had not been called back before firing commenced.

A few people ran out to the oasis to see if there was any damage.

Pvt. Richard Gibbons was shot several times but still alive. Pvt. Larry Knight was killed immediately.

The fire team leader who sent the two LP's out was never seen again, but who gave the orders to send them out in the first place?

Larry Knight's father came to the base and addressed our company. He told us that Larry was extremely proud to be a part of our unit and that he wanted to thank us all for befriending his son.

We stood silently listening to Mr. Knight. We all were thinking the same thing.

Capt. Clark and Sgt. Poe probably gave the orders to send out LP's and were ultimately responsible for the wounding of Pvt. Gibbons and the death of Pvt. Knight.

These are the people that are going to lead us in Vietnam? Heaven help us.

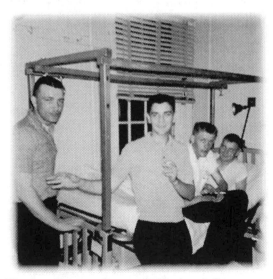

Danny Shain, Roger Bray, & Robert Spence, visiting
Richard Gibbons in the base hospital.

The Award

A short while after the ATTs were completed we had our normal morning formation. Sgt. Poe announced the results of the test. He announced the battalion awards: best company, not us; best commander, not Capt. Clark; best this and best that, none of which was "B" company.

Then he announced the best RTO in the battalion, but when he went to read the name he hesitated, finally he announced in a not so loud voice, "Pvt. Talerico." This time everyone in my platoon turned to look at me and congratulate me.

That was the only award our company received. Neither Capt. Clark nor Sgt. Poe ever said a word to me. However, Lt. Deems and Sgt. Corbett both came over to me and acknowledged it.

That was all I needed.

The Third Phone Call

After one Saturday inspection I was on my bunk reading my mail. My fire-team leader came upstairs and over to me.

He told me to get downstairs right away. The Company Commander was on a conference call with two congressmen and a senator wanting to know why I had not been transferred.

I ran downstairs again, praying they were still on the phone when I got there. When I arrived Sgt. Poe was standing behind his desk and my transfer papers were in front of him. He again told me to sign the papers, and I again refused.

He called me a coward. Now, if I were asking him to transfer me because I didn't want to go to Vietnam, then I could see him calling me a coward. But I wanted to stay with the 101st Airborne and I wanted to go with my unit to Vietnam, not because I wanted to go to war, but because it was my unit.

When he called me a coward, I looked him square in the eyes and said, "Why don't you come from behind your desk and we'll see who's a coward."

1st Sgt. Bobby R. Poe was relentless and I had just about all I could take from him.

He couldn't do any more than he was already doing to me so I didn't care. He just yelled some of his insulting ramblings, and then told me to get out of his office.

I just called home to inform them about the third call and how I was in more trouble.

Easter AWOL

Easter weekend, 1966, was nearing and I wanted to take a trip home. It had been a while and I didn't care about much of anything at this point. I told Steve Becsei I was going AWOL for the weekend.

He said he wanted to go with me because he never saw New York. When Friday rolled around we both took off and headed to Nashville. We hopped   plane and headed for New Jersey. We arrived Friday night around 8:00 pm.

We took a ride to NY so Becsei could see the city. We drove around for a while and got lost in some train yard. We finally made it back to my parent's home around 3:00 am.

The next night I got into a fight with some guy. I took all the anger I had from the last few months out on him. The next day, Easter Sunday, his parents came to my parent's home.

After a few minutes the father of the kid I fought informed me that he was a Lt Colonel in the 101st Airborne during WWII. He even invited me to his home the next day to look at his photos. It included the photo of Gen. Eisenhower with members of the 101st Airborne just prior to the invasion of Normandy, France, D-Day. He is the Lieutenant facing Gen. Eisenhower.

I thought for sure I was in big trouble, especially when he told me how he has a lot of friends still active. All are officers and high ranking at that. In the end, he didn't do anything. I often wonder if it was because I was in his old unit.

In the meantime, my new platoon leader, Lt. Mike Taylor, (Lt Deems was moved to Headquarters company, recon platoon), called my parents' home looking for Becsei and me.

When I spoke to him, he informed me that if we both returned tomorrow, nothing would happen to us. Both Becsei and I knew he was full of shit. We had planned on returning the next day anyway.

When we returned, Sgt. Poe told Becsei that he was busted to Pvt. E-2. Then he looked at me and held up my orders for promotion to Specialist E-4, then tore them up and busted me to Pvt. E-2. So I actually lost two ranks. I didn't care. I didn't care about anything at this point.

VIETNAM BOUND

The Ship

June 6, 1966, the sign of the beast (666), the same day as D-Day WWII, and two days before my 20th birthday, we set sail on the USS John Pope. We sailed out of Oakland Army Terminal, San Francisco. The Pope was a merchant marine ship used as a troop carrier in WWII.

There were about 2,000 troops on this ship, many from our battalion. The trip was to take eighteen days, all of which counted as combat time, and that was good.

We were a few decks below the main deck. Each squad had an area assigned to it. Each bunk had four beds with about eighteen inches of space above each bed. The squad leader was on the end bunk and the rest of the squad was in his row.

As you walked into the room, each bunk on the immediate right and immediate left was a squad leader's bunk. Each room held a platoon. So there were two rows of bunks on the right and two on the left. The squad leaders were at the open area where you walked in.

While passing under the Golden Gate Bridge, one of the ship hands was talking to us about our unit; he was about 50 years old and showed genuine interest in the airborne.

He told us that at the outbreak of WWII he too went under this bridge and was gone almost four years before he saw it again. He told us how when they went under the bridge everyone in his unit turned and saluted the bridge. When they returned, they did the same thing.

It was at that time that I made a vow to myself; "I will travel, either over or under this bridge again and salute it." At which point I looked at the bridge, stood at attention and saluted it. Several

91

others did the same thing.

There was a solemn quiet on deck. As I scanned the area, I thought to myself, "How many of us will be returning home in a coffin?"

We passed under the bridge and were on our way to war in a country called Vietnam.

Rifle Inspection

Once we were on our way I was immediately sent to the ships galley to report for KP. This was to be my job, every other day, for the duration of the trip.

It wasn't bad because the cooks were from the ship and they didn't hassle me at all. In fact they even let me off early because they didn't need me. Plus, they also didn't care for army officers.

In between KP, I was assigned to anything else that needed to be done. One day we were to have a rifle inspection. The rifles had to be brought up from five decks below and distributed to each squad.

Sgt. Leroy Thompson was assigned to the detail for our platoon and he needed someone to haul the rifles up the stairs of each deck. I was assigned the detail.

Sgt. Thompson and I went down the five decks to where the rifles were secured. He took the rifles out of the locked cases and handed them to me by squad. I then took the rifles, about eight to ten at a time and brought them up the skinny stairways to each squad leader.

After I finished bringing all our platoon's rifles up the stairs I was instructed to report to my squad and stand inspection. I went to my squad leader's bunk, grabbed my rifle and placed it on my bunk for inspection.

After the inspection was over Sgt. Thompson called for me and brought me back down to the rifle lockup. There, he told me to go upstairs and get the rifles off of each squad leader's bunk and bring them downstairs.

I went upstairs and grabbed the rifles off of each squad leaders bunk and brought them downstairs as ordered. After four trips up and down I waited for Sgt. Thompson to finish checking in all the rifles.

After a few minutes he looked at me and told me that one rifle was missing. He had to go through each rifle and check them in by serial number. When he was done, he told me that my rifle was missing and what was I trying to do? I went upstairs with him and sure enough, my rifle was still on my bunk.

While I was on detail I never placed my rifle on the squad leader's bunk and my squad leader never checked to make sure he had every member of his squad's rifle. It was an honest mistake, or perhaps a setup, but in any case it was not a big deal, or so I thought.

Sgt. Thompson was a buck Sgt, E-5, black, about 5' 10", and 180 pounds. He was the ideal soldier in our unit because he kissed the ass of everyone who outranked him. He was pathetic and Sgt. Poe loved him.

The airborne units have a large number of black soldiers. I came to realize that they went airborne to become something better while they served their country.

They took of pride in what they did and always did their best. They were much more "street smart" than the rest of us and didn't take shit from anyone. And when you needed a hand, they were there to help.

While in the platoon area with everyone standing around, Sgt. Thompson started to yell at me for screwing up again. He went on and on about how I'm always in trouble because of my bad attitude, etc., etc.

After a few minutes of his tirade I looked at him in the eye and intentionally said "Yes 1st Sgt, oops" at which point he pushed me with both hands.

I put up with Sgt. Poe and Capt. Clark for seven months, but it was only those two. No one else bothered me, and no one else belittled me. This Sgt. was a known ass-kisser and asshole.

After he pushed me in front of the platoon, I said "You fucking nigger" and punched him in the face. He went down, and while holding his chin he said "We got you now, you're going to be court-martialed for this."

I was placed under house arrest, which meant I could go anywhere on the ship, but I couldn't leave it.

I regretted using a racial slur. I should have called him incompetent, asshole, or anything else. From the deck, Sgt. Thompson looked around at the other black men, anticipating a reaction from them. Instead, they turned and walked away.

They had no respect for Sgt. Thompson either.

IN COUNTRY

Welcome to Vietnam

Early one morning we woke up and were told we arrived in Vietnam. We heard explosions outside the ship and thought we were under attack already. When we went topside we found troops throwing concussion grenades into the water. This was a preventive measure against any underwater attacks.

It was hot, about 110 degrees or at least it felt like it, plus it was very humid. Between the heat and the humidity I started getting a bad headache.

We got off the ship and loaded into trucks and were on our way. When we arrived at our destination the sign said "173rd Airborne."

We must have made a wrong turn somewhere because we were the 101st Airborne.

Our entire battalion from the 101st Airborne was now the 4th battalion, 503rd Infantry, 173rd Airborne Brigade, Separate. There were two infantry battalions from the 173rd already there, the 1st battalion and the 2nd battalion. There also was an artillery battalion. We were to be the 4th battalion.

After we arrived at base camp, we were assigned tents for each platoon. My squad leader told me that I was to put my equipment away and report to the CQ (Headquarters Tent).

Arrested, Maybe

I reported to HQ as ordered and there Sgt. Poe informed me that I was still under house arrest and I was to sit in a chair and be quiet. I did what I was told and sat quietly until they needed someone for KP or some other detail.

I didn't want to seem eager to go to KP, but I was actually looking forward to it. Sitting in a chair was boring and this was something to do.

After three days of this we finally were going to go out and do something. We were going on a training mission. It was to be in a secured area and its purpose was for us to get used to the heat and the jungle.

I was told to report to my platoon. I was given my rifle and my radio and went out like nothing ever happened. We were gone a few days and everything was normal. When we returned I went back under arrest and sat in HQ.

This went on a few times and there were no problems. I never understood how they could confine me while at base camp, but give me a rifle and better yet, a radio when there was an operation. I reported to my Plt. Ldr and assumed the responsibility of Plt. RTO.

Base camp – Bien Hoa

Pvt. Rayfon Lofton

The instructor told us that there should never be more than one man on the rope because it would stretch the rope too much and cause it to go below the water level.

Pvt. Ray Lofton was also in my company along with his friend Pvt. Joe Young. We didn't hang around together, but we were still friends. Ray was from Chattanooga, Tennessee. I don't know where Joe was from.

It was August 23, 1966; we were out on a mission. It was hot and humid, as we walked through the jungle we would sweat so much that our fatigues were soaking wet. Rain was a welcome relief and we got plenty of that. It rained all the time. Sometimes it rained for days at a time.

After a while we came upon a creek. We were told that we had to cross the creek. The creek wasn't more than twenty feet across, but it was moving at a fast pace.

It was already afternoon and we had been gone most of the day. Like in training one guy stripped down to his shorts, tied the rope around his waist and swam across to the other side of the creek. We tied the other end of the rope to a tree on our side and made sure the rope was taught.

The first person in our group got on the rope and started moving across the creek. Because of the speed of the creek it was slow going. Sgt. Poe came over and ordered the second guy to get on the rope.

The second guy got on the rope, causing it to stretch more, but it was still okay. Sgt. Poe ordered the third guy on the rope, even though there were two guys on the rope already. This is what we were told in training never to do.

This was Joe Young. While getting into the creek, he slipped and fell into the water. Two spotters, standing on the bank of the creek, reached down and grabbed hold of him and pulled him out of the creek, but not before he swallowed some water and was shaken up.

The first two guys were still on the rope. Lofton was next. Seeing his friend shaken up, Lofton took Young's helmet, backpack and rifle. Lofton turned to me, the next person to get on the rope after him and handed me Young's helmet and rifle.

The first person on the rope made it to the other side of the creek and climbed out. The second guy on the rope was in the middle of the creek.

When Lofton got on the rope and went into the creek he was carrying his rifle, his helmet, and two backpacks each weighing around 40 pounds. The rope stretched to the point where it was just above the water level not more than an inch or two, but way lower than what we trained for.

Instead of getting on the rope, I stood at the bank of the creek and pulled the rope so that Lofton would stay above water. I believed if I got on the rope with all my gear plus Young's helmet and rifle, plus my radio, Pvt. Lofton would go under.

It was working fine; Lofton started making his way across the rope. He reached the center of the rope with no problems. This was the swiftest part. With all the extra weight he started to show signs of fatigue. He wasn't making any progress. He was just holding on for dear life.

Sgt. Poe walked over and ordered me on the rope. I explained to him what I was doing, how Lofton was carrying extra weight and he would sink if I let go.

He didn't want to hear anything other than "Yes Sgt." I didn't let go. I held the rope firmly knowing that Lofton needed the help.

Unfortunately, Sgt. Poe wasn't listening to me. I was a lowly Private who was always in trouble. The thought of a Pvt. telling a 1st Sgt. anything was unthinkable. He never even looked at Ray

Lofton.

We started yelling at each other. I called him every name in the book. But my attention kept going back to the creek.

Lofton, in the meantime, wasn't moving and he was tired. Sgt. Poe was screaming things at me, but now I just ignored him. I was concentrating on Ray.

Hearing the commotion, Capt. Clark came over to see what the problem was. All Sgt. Poe told him was that I was refusing to get on the rope. I tried to tell Capt. Clark what was happening to Lofton but like Poe he didn't want to hear it.

He looked at me and said, "Get in the water or you will be court-martialed."

As soon as I let go of the rope, Lofton sank into the water over his head. I grabbed hold of the rope and pulled it back but it was too late. The spotters jumped into the water a few feet downstream but were unable to find Ray.

Sgt. Poe and Capt. Clark never said a word to me about the incident.

The next day, without me, my company went back to find Lofton and to cross the creek. They found him a little way down stream.

I think about this incident every day trying to convince myself that I was only following orders, but many years later when I started talking about it I realized something I never considered.

When Ray Lofton went under, in my panic, did I pull the rope out of his hands?

Did I cause his death?

OP Shoot to Kill

On our next mission we were guarding the battalion area in the field. This was a pretty easy job, especially since we were going to be there for a week or so.

Sgt. Poe instructed me and another private to go out about 75 meters and set up an LP position.

He instructed us to watch for anything. He also told us that there are no patrols in the area so if we see anything open fire and run back to the main area. That sounded stupid but we did as we were told.

I left my radio at my regular position and we walked out about 75 meters and set up our position.

This was not like the normal jungle. It was more like a forest. We were able to see about a hundred yards ahead with just a few trees blocking our view and not too many leaves at ground level.

About an hour after we set up we saw something. It looked like about five or six people walking through the woods in a single file.

The private I was with started aiming at the group and was getting ready to fire. After looking at them I thought that they might be some of our troops.

It looked like they were wearing helmets and camouflaged uniforms, the same as us. I told him not to fire because they might be ours. I told him I would run back and check with battalion to make sure no one else was out there.

When I ran back I got my radio and called battalion HQ. I asked if there were any patrols in our area. After a short pause their RTO came back and informed me that "A" Company had a patrol in our area.

I ran back to the LP position and let the other private know. If I had asked Sgt. Poe or Capt. Clark, they would probably be more concerned about me not being where I was told to be rather than their mistake.

This was a "non incident" that probably saved a few lives, including ours. But it was never recorded or even mentioned after that day. Capt. Clark and Sgt. Poe were now dangerous.

The Second Helicopter Ride

We were always on patrol. We would walk all day long and at night we would dig a foxhole. Then we took turns standing guard. Most times there were only two guys in each position. Therefore guard duty was half the night.

I hated Vietnam, more for the heat and humidity than the actual war. It was miserable, between the snakes, the scorpions, tarantulas, and the brush, it was a living hell. It was always raining during the monsoon season and hot and dry in the winter.

We knew where we were and we knew what was going on. Every once in a while we were reminded of the cold reality of war. One time, while on patrol, we went through a rice paddy.

We were walking along a ridge at the edge of a wooded area when we came upon a Vietnamese man. He was dead. He had his pants down and was bent like he was relieving himself.

A mortar must have hit him because his waist was blown away. The wound was a purple color and horrible. He must have been there a few days. Flies were all over him and buzzing around his body. I couldn't help thinking that he was probably an innocent person caught up in this senseless war like so many others.

Then one day we were told that we were going to go on "Eagle Flight". I had no idea what that meant, but when I heard "flight" I liked it.

Eagle flight is when a unit boards helicopters and flies around where our other units are on patrol.

If a unit gets in trouble, we were flown in to reinforce them. This sounded great; I didn't have to walk through the jungle. No sweating and no foxholes. Plus I got another chance to ride on a helicopter.

When the helicopters arrived I immediately went to the seat next to the machine gunner on the right side of the helicopter. A few things were different from my first helicopter ride back at Ft. Campbell.

For one thing I was carrying my radio under my backpack. When I climbed into the seat next to the door gunner I was sticking out of the helicopter a little. I wasn't too worried though, I would just strap in and everything would be fine.

I went to get the strap, but I couldn't find it. I asked the door gunner where it was. He informed me that there was no strap. No problem, I would just close the door and everything would be fine. When I went to close the door, it was stuck. I again informed the door gunner about the door this time. He told me the door is locked in the open position and to hang on as the helicopter took-off.

"Wait a minute! I'm hanging out of this thing! Holy shit! I'm going to fall out." Just then the helicopter banked right, I was literally holding both sides of the door trying not to fall out.

Boy was I scared, I thought for sure I was a goner. The helicopter finally straightened out and I was able to relax a bit. I was still outside the helicopter, but it wasn't anything like when we banked.

The flight was cool; we just flew around waiting for something to happen. Unfortunately, we were called into the middle of a firefight with the NVA. I don't know where we were or who was in trouble, but we went from cruising to top speed.

When we arrived at the area, the door gunner open fired into the area spraying rounds everywhere. He was clearing the area we were going into. I fired an M60 machine gun in AIT, but it was short bursts of 3 or 4 rounds each.

This time when the gunner open fired he was about a foot from my head and fired long bursts of gunfire. That noise, along with the helicopter was louder than anything I've experienced so far.

We were dropped in a rice paddy about five feet from the top of the paddy. When we arrived on the scene there was rifle fire going on and we joined in.

I don't know what happened. All I know is people were trying to shoot me.

I kept low and returned fire not knowing if I was shooting anywhere near the enemy. I just hoped we scared the hell out of them and they would run, and they did.

All helicopter rides after that were from inside the helicopter with the rest of the unit.

Stop from the Front

One day we were on another patrol. It was all of "B" company led by Capt. Clark, with Sgt. Poe by his side, near the front, but not too close to the front. I didn't know who was bringing up the rear and really didn't care. Our company was at full strength so the patrol was about one hundred strong with me somewhere in the middle.

Whenever a problem occurs at the front of the patrol, for whatever reason, it may have to stop. In order to avoid soldiers from closing in like an accordion we use a procedure to eliminate that from happening. The person in front should turn to the person directly behind him and say, "Stop from the front, pass it back." If the problem occurs at the end of the patrol, the last person should say to the person in front of him, "Stop from the rear, pass it forward."

This would help eliminate the accordion effect and keep the soldiers spread apart. This stopping of the patrol was not uncommon and didn't cause any problems.

One day, while on patrol, nature called and I had to go bad. It was becoming uncontrollable and something had to happen soon or I was going to go in my pants. I didn't know what to do.

Then I got an idea, I turned to the person behind me and said, "Stop from the front, pass it back." And he did. I turned to the person ahead of me and said, "Stop from the rear, pass it forward." And he did. The entire patrol came to a halt. I quickly stepped to the side of the path and did my business.

When I got back in line the person in front of me said, "The CO wants to know what the problem is?" I told the guy in front, "I don't know, but go from the rear." As soon as they started moving I told the guy behind me, "Go from the front." The patrol started moving.

I felt good, in more ways than one.

Sandbags

Whenever we went to the field, we carried with us a number of sandbags and our ponchos. The sandbags were used to fortify our positions. We would dig our foxholes, filling the sandbags at the same time.

The sandbags would go along the side and front of our foxhole. Then we would find trees, cut them down into logs and place the logs on top of the sandbags. If we had enough sandbags, we would put them on top of the logs.

This would sustain even a direct mortar hit. We used the ponchos when it rained. These two items kept us safe and dry.

We moved into an area and became "Palace Guards." We were guarding the battalion supply depot in the field. We were going to be there a couple of weeks so we dug in deep.

The only bad part of this area was it was very muddy. The ground was wet from all the rain and everything was a mess. Nevertheless we dug in. Fortunately water didn't fill our foxholes.

A friend of mine came over to tell me that his girlfriend had written him a letter and sent a photo. He grabbed his helmet with both hands and took it off his head and held it directly in front of him.

As soon as he could see inside the helmet he let out a yell and dropped the helmet to the ground. He said for me to look, and while we watched in horror, a scorpion walked out of his helmet. His girlfriend's letter may have saved his life.

After a short while, a private walked over to our position and said Sgt. Poe needs one poncho and six sandbags from each position. We didn't ask why, we just gave it to him.

Later on we found out why they needed our sandbags and ponchos. Fifty meters behind our perimeter Capt. Clark had privates fill our sandbags and create a sandbag floor for his tent. The tent was made using our ponchos.

He also had a sandbag floor made for the 1st Sgt's tent, again using our ponchos, and also for the engineer's tent, using more of our ponchos. Then there was a sandbag sidewalk going from Capt. Clark's tent to Sgt. Poe's tent and on to the engineer's tent. The sidewalk was about three feet wide.

These sandbags were carried out to the field for our protection. If that wasn't enough, Capt. Clark had two privates construct a sandbag wall the width of his tent, which slept two, and it was four feet tall.

It gets better. Capt. Clark then had an M60 machine gun mounted on his sandbag wall pointed to the perimeter and a machine-gunner on the machine-gun twenty-four hours a day.

If we had gotten into a firefight I believe he would have had the machine gunner fire right into our own guys.

Our XO (Executive Officer) 1st Lt. Mavroudis, shared the tent with Capt. Clark. It was rumored that he said he moved out of Capt. Clark's tent because Capt. Clark had a .45 pistol under his pillow, and he would cock it every five minutes.

The Crime

After digging my foxhole and filling the remaining sandbags we had left, I was called to report to Sgt. Poe. I figured it was some shit job and of course it was going to be mine.

When I reported to Sgt. Poe, he told me to dig a 5 by 5 to be used as the HQ foxhole. A 5 by 5 is a hole 5 feet wide, 5 feet long and 5 feet deep. I got my entrenching tool (shovel) and started to dig.

The ground wasn't hard and I was able to dig the hole in a short amount of time. When I was finished, Sgt. Poe walked over to me and told me to dig another hole to be used as a garbage dump.

I started digging the second hole as ordered. The second hole was as easy as the first and I was making good time digging it.

About three quarters of the way down Sgt. Poe and Capt. Clark walked over to me. I had completed my foxhole, their foxhole, and almost done with their garbage pit. It was hot and I was soaked with sweat, and extremely tired.

While I dug the first hole Sgt. Poe would walk by me and make remarks towards me. They were the usual comments and I learned to ignore him. That would piss him off even more and I loved it.

But this time the two of them came right up to the hole and started telling me things, like how to be a good soldier, how I should shape up and I wouldn't have any problems.

Instead of being smart and agreeing with them I stood up, dropped my entrenching tool, looked at Capt. Clark right in the eyes and I said these exact words, "Sir, I just hope you and I are never ever in a firefight together." At that moment I didn't care about anything.

Upon hearing what I said, Capt. Clark, in an excited voice, like he won a prize on "Let's make a Deal", said "That's it, we got you now, and you're going to be court-martialed."

They got what they wanted and I could care less. My only regret at this point was not taking that transfer and being on a beach in Monmouth, NJ.

When we returned to base I was back under arrest.

Capt. Clark in a surprise move, (he didn't have Sgt. Poe telling him what to say); read me something about my court-martial. I didn't hear a word he was saying because I was focused on how much I hated him.

I couldn't stand being near him. All I could think about was emptying a magazine into his big fat head and watching his brains splatter all over the tent wall.

Court Martial

Witnesses on my behalf were Lt. Deems and Pvt. Becsei. Lt Deems was no longer my platoon leader. He was reassigned within the battalion a while back.

Pvt. Becsei spoke about the things that happened back at Ft. Campbell. How things were good until Capt. Clark started getting phone calls about me, and how everything changed after that. Lt. Deems told about how I was the best RTO he ever had.

The one thing I remember most was when one of the judges asked Lt. Deems, while under oath, if after everything he heard, would he want me as his RTO now. Lt. Deems, without hesitation, said "Yes, I would take him with me anywhere." After hearing Lt. Deems say that, I realized that as a soldier I was okay, maybe even a little better than okay. It was all the bullshit from Sgt. Poe and Capt. Clark that poisoned my thinking.

During one of the breaks from the trial, Capt. Clark walked up to me and said "Don't worry; I know these officers and they are fair." He spoke to me as if he cared about me, in a friendly even reassuring voice. I knew then that these officers were going to stick together, especially if he knew them. I didn't trust him at all.

After about two minutes of deliberation, I was found guilty of insubordination. I was given the maximum sentence for this type of court-martial, six months at hard-labor in the stockade, loss of rank to E-2 again, and loss of two-thirds pay while in the stockade.

The only bright spot about the court-martial is that I would never have to hear from Capt. Clark or Sgt. Poe again.

LBJ Ranch

I arrived at the Long Binh Jail, better known as the LBJ ranch. It was a compound about four square acres and contained three large tents a mess hall and a headquarters tent. The guards, made up of MPs, also lived in the compound in their own tent.

When I arrived, it was late afternoon. I was assigned a bunk in one of the tents, and went to mess. After mess I wandered around a bit to see what this place was like. I noticed a group forming in the middle of the compound. I walked over and asked what was going on. Someone told me that they had a couple of marijuana joints.

Before I went to Vietnam I heard about marijuana. It was something the beatniks in Greenwich Village smoked to get high. I never saw it or knew anyone who smoked it.

When I got to Vietnam I started seeing some of the other guys smoking it. I never wanted to try marijuana because I heard that it makes you crazy. Several times in base camp guys would be smoking it and they would offer it to me. I was never interested in even trying it.

This time was different. I was in Vietnam, in the stockade. What else could they do to me? I asked for the marijuana joint and it was passed over to me. I took a drag and held it in like I was told to do. After a few seconds I exhaled and became a little dizzy.

At that moment I heard the last thing I wanted to hear, over the PA system, I heard, "Pvt. Talerico, report to the company commander's tent." All I could think of was how did they know I was smoking a joint and what about everyone else who was smoking? I didn't know what I looked like. Would the CO see I was high?

I was scared of what was about to happen. When I arrived at the CO's tent, I approached his desk and stood at attention. I had no idea what I looked like. Could he tell I was high? I didn't feel any different, but I thought how would I know? He welcomed me to the jail. Then he told me about a few rules and how if I just stay out of trouble my time would pass smoothly. He didn't know I was high. I didn't know I was high. In fact I wasn't high at all.

After hearing my name on the PA system, I must have sobered up instantly. Anyway, I left his tent and went back to find out what this marijuana stuff was supposed to do.

The MPs at the stockade were all unhappy with their assignment. The last thing they wanted to do, while in Vietnam was to guard soldiers in the stockade. They were also sympathetic to us because they knew where we came from, mostly the infantry. They would never give us a hard time.

One time an MP took five of us out to do our "hard labor," breaking up this giant boulder. It was about five feet tall and about as wide. Our job was to break it up. We marched out of the compound to the boulder, which was about a half-mile away from the compound.

The MP told one of the guys who brought a sledgehammer to use it on the rock. The prisoner took the sledgehammer and hit the rock as hard as he could. Nothing happened, not even a chip came off the rock. Then the MP told a different guy to hit the rock. After the second guy hit the rock the MP told the third guy to hit the rock.

We began to understand what he was doing. We all took turns hitting the rock one time. After that he told us to sit down and relax, that we had to stay out of the compound a few hours before we could return. He did his job. We all took turns hitting the rock. We found a few trees and relaxed for the remaining time of the detail.

The stockade wasn't going to be too bad, other than the fact that "stockade time" had to be made up in Vietnam. This meant that I would be spending a year and a half here instead of one year, which sucked.

The great majority of the guys in the stockade were from the infantry. Some of their crimes were really bad. One guy threw a pickaxe at his guard and hit him right in the forehead, while under arrest.

Another guy hung his 1st Sgt. and strangled his company commander; I should have made friends with him. One guy emptied a magazine into his squad leader while he was sleeping. This war was making people crazy. The list goes on and on. I thought to myself, "These guys are serious criminals, what am I doing here with them?" I did my best to stay away from most people there.

The Noose

After a few days I met a guy named Rick, which is all I can remember. He was a psychologist back in the "world" and was in the stockade for going AWOL. It seems he was gone for ninety days before the boyfriend of a girl he was seeing turned him in.

He told me how he survived by using the black market. When they finally got him, he had over a thousand dollars and all new civilian clothes. He also got six months in the stockade. We became friends and he slept on the cot next to me.

One day while sitting on our cots talking I happened to have a piece of cord. One of my uncles back in NJ once showed me how to make a noose. Not for any reason, just for fun.

As Rick and I were talking I began to make a noose with this piece of cord. When mess was called we both got up and went to eat. I tossed the noose on Rick's cot not thinking anything about it.

The stockade in Vietnam was about sixty percent black. A few days later I heard that Rick was in trouble. Apparently, a black guy saw the noose on Rick's cot and assumed it was something to do with blacks in general.

They were planning to do something to Rick. When I heard this I went out to the compound and saw a large group (approximately fifty) of black guys standing around. I walked up to them and asked about the problem with Rick and the noose.

They told me it was a KKK thing and they didn't like it and were going to do something about it. I told them it was my noose that I made and it had nothing to do with blacks. I wasn't too scared because the guards were watching from about twenty yards away and saw everything that was going on. If they weren't watching I wouldn't be there. After a few minutes I convinced them that I was telling the truth.

I remember walking back to my tent. Rick was waiting for me to return. When I walked in he asked me what happened. I told him everything was okay and he had nothing to worry about. That began to make me realize how much blacks had to put up with over the last centuries. Blacks represent ten percent of the army and sixty percent of the stockade. Something wasn't right.

Inspector General

At the completion of my second week in the stockade, the Inspector General, a major in the 173rd Airborne, visited me. He informed me that he visits everyone from the 173rd as standard procedure, said it would only take about one-half hour or so.

I sat at a table across from him. No one else was in the tent and he told me to forget his rank and to speak freely.

I proceeded to tell him about being a good RTO and that until that first phone call, everything was going great. After that first phone call I was given extra details because I refused to sign papers transferring me to Ft. Monmouth.

I explained how I was treated like shit because I wanted to stay with my unit. How it didn't make any sense to me. I went on and on.

By the time we were done, he asking me questions, me telling my story, three hours had passed.

He told me it was the longest he had ever spent with anyone. Then he said that he was hoping to get his own infantry company and would like me to be his driver. I asked him why me?

He said I was crazy enough not to run when the firing started. I laughed and said "Sir, why would I run, I have the jeep, just make sure you are in it at the time."

I was released from the stockade the following week. Upon my release I received a check for $53 from the Chase Manhattan Bank. I had no idea why the check was not military script.

All I cared about was being out of the stockade.

1st Battalion, "A" Company

"Welcome to Camp Ray, Home of the 1st Battalion, 173rd Airborne", the sign said. It already looked better than the 4th Battalion. The one thing the 4th Battalion had was Colonel "Iron Mike" Healy, a hard-nosed leader whom we all respected and liked.

I didn't know who was commanding this battalion. One thing I knew was this battalion had been here since the beginning and had a fierce reputation.

My orders were to report to "A" Company. When I arrived at "A" company I reported to the CQ as ordered. I was told the unit was in the field and I was to get settled and that I would go out with the next morning mess. I unpacked my duffle bag and got settled in. I thought of this as a new start. I didn't know anyone, but that was okay.

After settling in I took a walk around the company area. It was good to be out of the stockade, especially after only a few weeks instead of six months. I must have made a good impression on the inspector general. I hoped he'd get his company.

I asked the clerk where I could get my $53 check cashed. He said he didn't know, but the CO would know. I waited to see him.

Nine Jump Commands

The next morning I got my gear ready and went to the mess tent.
They were preparing to go to the field with the morning mess so I
helped load the helicopters.

We took off and after a short while we arrived at "A" company. I
reported to the CO and he assigned me to the 1st platoon.

When I arrived at the platoon area I saw something strange going
on. Everyone was standing around the edge of a crater created
by a 1,000-pound bomb. Standing on the edge was the medic.

During the previous night, while on guard at their position, two
guys heard something in the bush ahead of them.

When they realized they were hearing two guys speaking
Vietnamese, they knew immediately that it was VC. They opened
fire and killed both of them. By morning rigor mortis had set in and
both VC were stiff.

While one guy was taking pictures, the medic took one VC at a
time, stood him up at the edge of the crater, put a smile on his
face, and started the nine jump commands. "Get Ready", by this
time everyone was repeating what the medic was yelling, "Stand
Up", all the way to "Stand in the Door", at this point he bent the
VC's knees, moved both arms to each side as if he was holding
the door of the airplane, then he yelled "Go".

He then pushed the VC down into the crater. After a lot of
cheering he did the same with the second VC. This time everyone
was yelling in sync with the medic.

When both bodies were down the bottom of the crater the medic
took a grenade and tossed it in the crater. When it went off the
explosion caused the sides of the crater to collapse enough to
cover the two VC.

I remember thinking how this war is really screwed up. Are we the "good guys"?

Saigon

When we returned from the field, I went over to the CQ and asked to speak to the CO. I asked him where I could cash the $53 check I received from the stockade.

He told me that Sgt. Jackson goes to Saigon a few times a week and I could catch a ride with him. I found Sgt. Jackson and told him my situation. He said I could go the next day with him.

Sgt. Jackson and I arrived in Saigon late morning. He showed me where the Chase Manhattan bank was and then brought me to the Ambassador Hotel. He dropped me off in front of the main entrance of the hotel.

There was a stairway going up to the main entrance. Sgt. Jackson told me that he would be there at 4:00 pm and that I should be there waiting for him. If I wasn't there he couldn't wait for me. I understood and went on my way.

The first thing I did was head to the bank to cash my check.

Saigon was a large city, but it was dirty. Everyone rode bicycles. Hundreds of them were on every street. There were also a lot of rickshaws being pulled by little men with wide straw hats.

Small cars, mostly Volkswagens, were fighting to get through the crowded streets. There was a lot of noise coming from the horns of the cars, and people were shouting all different things in Vietnamese.

I went to get a haircut at a barbershop on the street. I was waiting for my turn for a haircut when I noticed a barber ask the Vietnamese customer something. The customer acknowledged.

The barber took hold of the man's head with one hand on his chin and the other hand on the back of his head and slowly started to turn his head from side to side. Then with a quick twist, he turned his head and you could hear the man's head snap.

The man got up and paid the barber, smiled and went on his way. Now it was my turn. I got my haircut, when the barber was finished he asked me something in Vietnamese. I didn't understand the words, but I knew what he was asking. There was no way I was going to let some Vietnamese snap my neck. Who knows what he would do? Maybe he was VC. I paid the man and left the shop.

I continued aimlessly through the streets of Saigon. There were many different sights to see. The culture was completely different from what I was used to in the States. The food vendors on the streets were selling anything and everything.

There were dead chickens that were plucked but had the heads still on. There were all different kinds of fish, from squid to things with the eyes hanging out of them. It was definitely different but somehow kind of neat.

By 2:30 I had spent all of the $53. With nothing left to do, I started towards the Ambassador Hotel. When I arrived at the hotel the time was 3:00 pm, an hour before Sgt. Jackson was to meet me.

I had a great day and now it was back to "A" company. Four o'clock rolled around and no Sgt. Jackson.

Four thirty...five o'clock...five thirty and still no Sgt. Jackson.

AWOL in Saigon

Different things were going through my head. My biggest concern was "are they setting me up"? Was this planned from the very beginning? I was worried that I was going to Ft. Leavenworth. I didn't know what to do.

My first thought was to find an MP or someone who could help get me back. But then I thought that would be playing right into their hands. It was starting to get dark and I didn't want to be outside at night in Saigon. I found a hotel and went inside.

I spent all the money I had but I remembered my friend Rick from the stockade telling me about the black market and how he made a lot of money. I went up to the desk and approached the clerk.

He was a middle-aged Vietnamese man and was very polite. He spoke English with a Vietnamese accent. I told him of my predicament and how if he gave me a room I would go to the PX (Post Exchange) and get him whatever he wanted tomorrow.

He was not interested. In fact he was adamant about it. I knew I was in trouble. I tried for several minutes to convince him but to no avail.

Then a man sitting in the lobby, listening to my conversation with the clerk, came up to the counter and asked me what the problem was. He was an American and also a civilian. He worked at one of the construction companies in Saigon.

He was a little older than me and his name was Ray. After telling him my story, Ray got me aside and told me about the black market and how there were four army PXs and one navy PX in Saigon.

I told him I heard about the black market and how it could make someone a nice profit, but I wasn't sure how to do it. He paid for my room and told me to meet him in the lobby in the morning.

I went to my room and thought about the trouble I was in. I kept thinking that somehow, with this entire war going on, that the army had some kind of conspiracy against me. And now I was AWOL for the second time. I finally fell to sleep.

The next morning I went down to the lobby and Ray was waiting for me. We had breakfast together and he told me how the black market works.

All the cab drivers have military ration cards. If you go in a cab and ask them to take you to a PX, they will ask you to buy them something. They will give you the cost of what they want in military script (Army Money). When you return with their product they will pay you the same amount of money also in military script. It seemed like a pretty easy thing to do and no one gets hurt.

Off I went

Black Market

I found a cab and climbed in. I asked the driver to take me to the PX. Exactly like Ray said, the cab driver turned his head towards me and asked "You go PX, you buy me something?" to which I said yes.

He took me to the nearest PX and parked at the corner of the street. He told me that they were not allowed to pull in front of the PX. They could only go to the corner.

He said he would be going around the block because they couldn't wait either. He would pick me up at the same corner when I return.

He asked me to buy him two cartons of cigarettes and gave me the money in military script plus his illegal ration card. Two cartons was the maximum allowed with the ration card. I went inside the PX and purchased his cigarettes.

The clerk behind the counter took my ration card and checked off the cigarettes. When I returned to the corner, the cab driver was already there.

I gave him the cigarettes and his ration card. He took the cigarettes and placed them under his seat. Then he took what looked like a small bottle of a clear liquid from his pocket.

He opened the bottle and dipped a Q-tip in it, then gently wiped the check marks the clerk in the PX made. The check marks disappeared in a few moments.

He gave me the equivalent amount of money for the purchase and asked if I wanted to go to another PX. I told him that I would.

We continued on and hit all the army PXs. By the end of the day I had about $50. I paid Ray back for the money he loaned me and paid for another night at the hotel.

The next day I repeated the process. I was going along with the black market business the second day, but it was starting to bother me.

Was I somehow funding the VC? I started to think the profits these guys were making might have supported the VC so I changed tactics. When the cab drivers would drop me off with their ration card and their military script I did something different.

Instead of purchasing what they wanted, I would walk slowly towards the PX entrance. Instead of entering the PX, I would run to the other end of the block and get into another cab. Once in the second cab, I would ask to go to another PX, and it would start all over again.

By the end of the second day I made close to $100. The only thing I had to worry about was getting into a cab I already ripped off. There were thousands of cabs in Saigon and I knew the odds were in my favor.

MP Guard

By the second night I was less afraid of Saigon. I was making money, eating well and buying some new civilian clothes. That night I saw a movie theater and decided to check it out.

Outside was a bunker, surrounded by sandbags and guarded by an American MP. I walked up to the MP and started talking to him. I told him I was on R&R (Rest and Recuperation) in Saigon for a few days. He seemed interested in the 173rd and asked a lot of questions about things he heard in the infantry.

After a while he asked me if I would like to join him and the other MPs for a continental breakfast at his hotel. I agreed, thinking to myself "What, am I crazy?" But, the next morning I was eating a great breakfast with about a hundred MPs.

After breakfast I went on my way. I stopped by his guard post at the movie a couple of times that day and talked to him for a while. He was a nice guy and I thought of turning myself in to him, but not yet.

The Grandkids Story

In my wanderings around Saigon I came upon a harbor. I knew Vietnam bordered on the ocean, but I didn't know Saigon was a major harbor. I walked around the harbor for about an hour when I came upon a large ship.

It wasn't a navy ship but it was big. I saw a ship hand working near the dock and I asked him where the ship was heading. He told me that they were getting ready to set sail for Singapore.

I started to think, "I'm going to go back to the stockade, this time for a long Time. What if I was able to hop this ship and work my way to Singapore? Then over the next few years I could work my way back to the States? What a great story to tell my grandkids. It seemed like it could work.

I asked the ship hand if they were hiring and he told me they are always hiring. He pointed to the top cabin on the ship where the captain was. He is the only one who can hire.

I walked up the gangplank and proceeded up to the main cabin. When I knocked on the door I saw an older gentleman with white hair and a white beard. He was short and chubby and was having dinner with a woman. He was wearing a white navy type uniform and I assumed he was the captain.

He asked what I wanted. I told him I was looking for work and I understood that they were heading for Singapore. I was wearing civilian clothes so he asked if I was in the service.

At first I wanted to say no, but I told him I was in the army, but AWOL. He told me immigration comes aboard and checks the ship thoroughly and he could lose his job if I were caught. I understood and thanked him for listening then walked out of there.

If he said that I could work the ship, I would have been gone in a heartbeat. Instead the time was nearing to turn myself in.

The Surrender

On the fourth day in Saigon I decided to turn myself in to the MP I made friends with. I found him at his post around noontime. When I told him I was AWOL he was surprised.

He told me to wait there until the end of his guard duty. About an hour passed when he was relieved. By this time I told him my life story and he seemed sympathetic towards me.

He took me to see his Sgt. in charge and explained to the Sgt. how I got stuck in Saigon. They placed me in a jail cell, but left the door open. I was told they contacted my company and that they were sending someone to get me.

About an hour later a Sgt. from my company arrived. No papers were signed, which seemed a little strange for the army, and we were on our way back to Camp Ray.

When I returned to "A" company, I was told to report to the CO. I didn't know what to expect. I wasn't told I was under arrest or anything like that, but I was scared. I thought I was going back to the stockade for sure.

When I reported to the CO he immediately told me to stand at ease. He then told me that when I didn't show up for roll call the next morning, Sgt. Jackson told the CO he forgot to pick me up.

I wasn't in any trouble. I wasn't even considered AWOL. Sgt. Jackson openly admitted forgetting to pick me up as soon as he realized I was missing. This was strange. A Sgt. who openly admits something I did wrong was his fault, and an officer who listens?

Then the CO asked me something else. He asked me if I would like to be the Battalion messenger. I didn't know what that was, but it sounded good.

He explained that I would be driving a jeep for the Battalion adjutant and I would not be going back to the field. I jumped on that. I was to report to Capt. Decanto immediately.

Goodbye jungle, hello coasting time.

Battalion Messenger

I was assigned my own jeep and my job was to be the driver for anyone in the adjutant's office. The battalion adjutant was Capt. Decanto from New York. The assistant adjutant was Lt. Pleasants. The NCOIC (non-commissioned officer in charge) was Sgt. Bennet. And the clerk was Spec. 4 Mike Hardin.

When I wasn't driving anyone I would do odd jobs around the office. The thing I liked best was that I didn't need a shovel. No more foxholes, 5 x 5's, or ditches to dig, I had it made. I liked this job a lot and the rest of my tour was going to be cake.

Capt. Decanto

Capt. Decanto was a company commander before he became adjutant. He was a good guy and we all liked him. He was all army and by the book, but he was fair. He was from NYC and that was a good thing.

About twice a week Capt. Decanto would have me drive him to "Admin Alley". The 173rd Airborne Brigade was headquartered inside the Bien Hoa airbase.

The best way to describe the brigade area is like a wheel. The wheel has four spokes with a battalion at each end. In the middle of the wheel is "Admin. Alley" where brigade headquarters, the brigade hospital, and the officer's clubs are situated.

To get to "Admin Alley" we had to pass through a minefield about two miles long. The only road going through this minefield was secure and there was a guard post about halfway through. Two Vietnamese soldiers manned this guard post at all times.

Lt. Pleasants

The assistant adjutant was Lt. Pleasants. He was a young officer and was pretty cool. He always had a smile and was usually in a good mood.

The only time he went to admin alley was at night. He liked going to the officer's club at admin alley because that's where the nurses were.

Sgt. Bennet

The NCOIC was Staff Sgt. Bennet. For some reason we didn't hit it off like the others. He was a lifer and he didn't care much for me. I was drafted and a lot of lifers don't like draftees. He knew I didn't want to be in the army. I had to be there. He was an older man, probably in his forties. I knew to be careful around him, and I was, almost.

Spec. 4 Mike Hardin

The battalion clerk was Spec. 4 Mike Hardin. He was about my age, maybe a year or two older. We hit it off right away. We were the only two guys in the office who had little rank. Mike was a funny guy, not with jokes, but with his demeanor. He always said things that, by themselves, wouldn't be funny, but the way he would say them made you laugh.

Mike also had the ability to write passes for people to go off base to Bien Hoa. This came in handy quite often.

Vietnamese Guard post

The road to admin alley had a few interesting features. First it was the only way to get to admin alley, and second, it had a Vietnamese outpost.

The significant thing about the outpost was that you could get marijuana cigarettes there. A pack of cigarettes with the tobacco removed and replaced with marijuana was $2.

I don't know about the officers or the NCOs, but pretty much everyone else smoked marijuana. Some brought it to the field with them, but most guys didn't.

When I pulled up to the guard post I would point to my head with my index finger and move it in a circular motion, at the same time say, "Dinky dow cigarettes?" As soon as I would do that they knew exactly what I wanted.

Out came a pack of cigarettes, usually Marlboro reds. I would give them $2 in script and be on my way. After a few days I would recognize them and they me and I didn't have to say anything.

Bien Hoa

When I was in the 4th battalion I never got to go to the town of Bien Hoa. As 1st battalion messenger I went to Bien Hoa many times.

The best way to describe Bien Hoa is like the worse ghetto possible. The streets are lined with shacks and old single story buildings that look as though they were about to collapse.

The three main businesses along the main strip were laundries, bars, and "short time" houses. A "short time" house is where you can be with a woman for $2. After the 1st Division (Big Red One) moved into the area the price went up to $3. Leave it up to "Legs" to raise the price.

The bars were always full of GI's. There was always a lot of yelling and hollering about who was the best. Even with all the competitiveness about who was the best, there were never any fights. We knew that we were all in this war together. It was fun and a great release.

If you wanted to buy a girl a drink they would sit with you. Their drinks were non-alcoholic tea. We paid the same price as our drinks even though it was tea. This way they could get the GI's to keep buying more and more.

This was working out just fine. Mike Hardin would write the pass for both of us and I would drive the jeep. We went to Bien Hoa a few times a week; life was good.

ROK Truck Overload

One day I was downtown Bien Hoa looking to get my jeep painted. It was a great deal and I knew other drivers who had recommended this paint shop. To paint the entire jeep and even repaint the numbers would cost me $20. I decided to go ahead and have it done.

While waiting for the jeep to be painted I noticed a commotion across the street, about 50 yards down the road. It seems a ROK (Republic of Korea) Lieutenant and an American Lieutenant were arguing.

I saw some other GI's looking on and they were closer than I was, so I walked over to them. I asked them what they were arguing about and they told me the American lieutenant was telling the Korean lieutenant that he had too many prisoners on the truck.

The truck's maximum capacity was eighteen and there were nineteen prisoners. Ninety-nine percent of officers in the army would have cared less about one too many people on the truck. This army officer felt he was going by the book and was not going to give in.

We heard stories about the South Korean Army, or ROKs, as they were known. One of the stories I remember was their AWOL rate. It was one of the lowest in the world.

If you go AWOL, the first time you receive six months at hard labor, not like us, real hard labor. The second time they hang you in front of your battalion. I don't know if this is true or not, but they were much stricter than we were.

The ROK officer was getting angrier and wanted to move out, but the army officer, in a more reserved, even uppity manner told the ROK, "NO". The ROK officer, totally frustrated, reached into the truck and pulled out the closest prisoner to him.

Without saying a word, he dragged the prisoner over to an open rain barrel, which was filled to the brim with water and shoved the prisoner; head first, into the barrel. The prisoner fought to get free, but the officer held him until he stopped fighting.

As he walked past him, the ROK made some comment to the army officer, who was standing with his mouth wide open and speechless. We were stunned, but this went along with what we heard about ROKs.

Old King Cole

One afternoon, Lt. Pleasants told me to have the jeep ready for him after dinner. He wanted me to take him to admin. alley, specifically the officer's club at the hospital. I informed Mike Hardin and he wrote a couple of passes.

After mess, I met Lt. Pleasants and drove him through the minefield, past my friends at the guard post, and to the hospital officer's club. When I dropped him off he told me to pick him up at ten thirty.

As soon as I dropped him off I headed back to the 1st Batt to pick up Mike Hardin and the two of us headed downtown to Bien Hoa.

Mike liked to drink and this night was no exception. I drank a little, but not much because I was driving, and also I had to pick up Lt. Pleasants. We also bought a pack of "cigarettes" from the Vietnamese guards on the way out. Even though I wasn't drinking much, I was pretty high.

The 173rd base camp was inside the Bien Hoa airbase. There were two checkpoints, one for the airbase manned by AP (Air Police), and one for the 173rd manned by MPs. The airbase and the 173rd curfew was ten thirty.

We hit a few bars and also a few short time houses during the night. We were having a great time. While in a short time house Mike realized how late it was and told me we had to go. We hardly had enough time to make it back.

I jumped up and threw my clothes on, slipped into my boots and headed out the door with Mike.

We rushed back to the airbase and made it in time. I was buttoning my shirt while speeding back to the 173rd checkpoint. We were late. A line of jeeps and a few trucks were waiting to get past the MPs.

A few of the vehicles had to pull over to the side because they were past curfew and had to be reported. I was still trying to finish getting dressed, especially now that we are going to be checked.

Our turn was next. I pulled up and turned off the jeep as instructed. The MP approached the jeep and looked in with a flashlight. He noticed the way we were dressed and then he asked for my Id. I was in trouble again. I knew it. This time I had no one to blame but myself.

I gave the MP, his name was Finkel, my ID and he looked at it with his flashed. After a few seconds he asked me where I was from.

I was a little surprised, why would he want to know that? I told him I was from New Jersey. He then asked me what town I lived in. I said Little Falls. Then he asked me if I had any relatives in North Caldwell.

Feeling a lot better, I said yes, my cousin Joe and Jimmy Talerico. He looked at me and said in a friendly voice, "I went to West Essex High School with Jimmy." We chatted for a minute or so, and then he told me to go ahead.

I have a lot of cousins, many whom I truly love, but that moment in time elevated my cousin Jimmy Talerico right to the top of my list. I will be forever grateful to Jimmy. He is a great guy, well liked, funny, and good hearted.

We headed to the officer's club to pick up Lt. Pleasants. When we arrived it was about ten forty-five. We were late. I stuck my head in the door and told the first person I saw to let Lt. Pleasants know his driver was here. Lt. Pleasants came out with another Lt. and two nurses.

He ordered me to drive the nurses to their barracks so I did. Lt. Pleasants and the other Lt. and two nurses sat in the back. Mike Hardin, who wasn't supposed to be there, was riding shotgun.

143

As we drove to the nurse's quarters the two Lieutenants started singing. They were all drunk, the lieutenants, the nurses, and especially Mike Hardin.

Mike started singing along with the officers. I was laughing my butt off. It was the funniest thing I've seen Mike do. They were singing the officer's words, but he didn't care, and the officers didn't know.

When we arrived at the nurse's quarters, Lt. Pleasants walked the nurses to their door. While he was gone, Mike got out of the jeep and walked across the road to relieve himself. It was dark out, but you could see a fence on the other side of the road.

It was a wooden fence, like a corral type. The posts in the ground were about six to eight inches in diameter. While Mike was relieving himself and the other Lt. was still singing we heard a very loud groan, like someone was trying to move something extremely large. The other Lt. and I didn't have any idea what it was.

A few minutes later Mike showed up, we asked him what the noise was and he said, "The post was in my way, I had to move it." As soon as Lt Pleasants returned we took off. The singing resumed and nothing ever was mentioned about us being late, or the post.

The Letter Home

Of all the things I regret in my life, this is one of the things I regret the most.

After a few weeks as battalion messenger, Capt. Decanto called me into his office. He had me stand at attention and was visibly angry. I had no idea what could possibly be wrong.

He asked me one question, "When was the last time I wrote a letter home?" Surprised at the question, I told him I didn't know for sure, probably a few weeks. He said, "How does eleven weeks sound?" I was surprised by his response.

He told me that he was contacted by the Red Cross and that my mother was frantic because she hadn't heard from me.

I was young and stupid. I was only thinking about myself, about the fear and frustration of being in Vietnam, the stockade, Capt. Clark and Sgt. Poe, and many other things. I hated being there and all I could think about was going home. I never liked writing letters and I never knew what to say when I did.

My mother, knowing how I didn't like writing, would send me self-addressed postcards that read some simple message. All I had to do was sign and mail them so she knew I was alive.

It could have not been any easier. My Aunt Margaret and Aunt Ida would drive ten miles every day to check my mother's mail and call her at work to let her know if anything had arrived from me.

I never thought about my mother's younger brother Bobby Pepe who was killed in WWII. We were the same age while at war. I never realized how she must have felt.

Capt. Decanto ordered me to go in the other room and write a six-page letter, both sides, to my mother right now. When I was finished I was to give it to him to read and make sure I didn't say anything he thought was stupid or out of place. I wrote the letter and made sure I wrote home often after that.

As I get older I realize more and more how much pain I must have caused my Mother and it has never stopped hurting.

The Ambush

When I was court-martialed my RTO duties were turned over to Pvt. Frank Lee Smith. Frank was a nice, soft-spoken guy who got along with everyone.

He was in my platoon back at Ft. Campbell and deployed with the battalion to Vietnam.

One day, while driving to admin alley to drop off some papers, I decided to go to the 4th battalion area to see if anyone I knew was there. It was late January 1967.

When I arrived, I saw Roger Bray and Steve Becsei. They told me about an ambush that took place a week or so earlier. On January 16, 1967, the third platoon was on patrol, with Sgt. Thompson in charge. Pvt. Frank Smith was the RTO and Pvt. Lowman Abraham was second in command.

While on patrol they were ambushed by VC. Frank Smith was shot and killed immediately, Sgt. Thompson, true to form, hit the ground giving the platoon no direction.

The guy we all thought would be the first to run took charge of the situation, Pvt. Lowman Abraham. From what I was told, Pvt. Abraham stood firm, firing his rifle with one hand and his pistol with the other.

He was yelling out orders while Sgt. Thompson hugged the ground. I don't know if Pvt. Abraham received any medals but I do know he proved everyone who doubted him wrong. He talked a lot about what he was going to do while back in the States, and he did everything he said.

Pvt. Lowman Abraham backed up every word he ever said. He never hesitated for one second to act.

He was big and he was mean in Kentucky. In the end he was big and he was mean in Vietnam, and I'm glad he was on our side.

As for Pvt. Frank Lee Smith, I could only think of one thing. It could have been me.

FNGs

Every once in a while a truck full of FNGs (Fucking New Guys) would arrive at battalion headquarters. We would know ahead of time when they were coming.

Mike Hardin and I, along with anyone in the area, would wrap ourselves in bandages and just happen to be in the vicinity of where the truck would stop. When the FNGs would pull up in their truck we would be walking around the area.

Sometimes we had crutches and even wheelchairs. The look on their faces was priceless. We would walk up to the new guys and welcome them to the 1st battalion. It was a mean thing to do, but it was far less than the reality of what they were facing.

If anyone was a shortimer (someone with a few days to go in Vietnam) they would wear a playing card, changing the card as each day would go. The card would be equal to the number of days they have left in country.

If you had five days left, you wore a five. You simply cut a slit in the center of the card and put a button through it.

One guy had his nametag on his shirt changed to "Shortimer." He had people thinking that was his name.

The Screw up

Every night one of the Sgts. in our battalion would be assigned to courtesy patrol. This is where they go downtown Bien Hoa with a truck, at the end of the evening and pick up any GIs from the 173rd.

It's a way of keeping the drunks from forgetting to return and therefore be AWOL. Nothing usually happens to these GIs. They are returned with no repercussions.

About a week later, Mike Hardin and I went to downtown Bien Hoa as usual. Mike wrote the pass for both of us and signed Sgt. Bennet's signature.

We were in the Cherry Bar, a place we frequented often, having a grand old time. We were sitting in the back of the bar which was not too visible from the front. We had a few too many drinks and were carrying on about everything and anything.

To our surprise, we saw Sgt. Bennet walk in the bar. He was on courtesy patrol and looking for drunks. Instead of shutting our mouths, sinking in our chairs so he wouldn't see us, we started calling out to him.

Mike and I both were waving, trying to get his attention. When he saw us, he walked back to where we were and told us to get back now and report to him in the morning. We were in trouble, both of us.

The next morning we both reported to Sgt. Bennet as ordered. Mike was in trouble for forging the passes and I was in trouble for using a forged pass, but worse, taking my jeep off the base without authorization.

We were both busted, Mike to PFC and I was busted to Pvt. E-2, again. Mike was the battalion clerk. He knew all the jobs that had to be done in the battalion, and he was needed. On the other hand, I drove a jeep, a job that anyone could do, and therefore not needed.

I was transferred to reconnaissance platoon, and that did not sound good.

Recon was a proud unit and usually spearheaded any battalion operation. I wasn't happy about this at all, plus they were down to about twenty guys. Way below platoon strength.

I figured I was going to spend the remaining four months in this platoon so I'd better make the best of it.

Recon Platoon

I reported to recon platoon, HQ Company, 1st Battalion, 173rd Airborne. I quickly learned about this platoon.

They were the first army unit to arrive in Vietnam. They were involved in the battle to secure the Bien Hoa airbase. The battle for Bien Hoa, Operation Hump, November 8th, 1965, was one of the fiercest battles in Vietnam. The battalion was overrun by 1200 VC. The unit suffered many casualties.

The 173rd established itself as a top fighting unit and one of the best the US Army had to offer, and this was the only platoon in the entire Vietnam War to have three Medal of Honor winners, Spec. 4 Alfred Rascon, Sgt. Larry Pierce and Spec. 6 Lawrence Joel.

Recon was a proud unit and usually spearheaded any battalion operation. I wasn't happy about this at all, plus they were down to about twenty guys. Way below platoon strength.

I figured I was going to spend the remaining four months in this platoon so I'd better make the best of it.

The Perfect Logs

Early February 1967 we were on patrol as usual. The jungle was particularly thick and we had been walking all day. It stopped raining and we were nearing our destination.

We arrived at a large clearing about two acres of clear land. Next to the clearing was a forest of perfectly straight trees.

The trees were about twenty feet tall, but the trunks were about eight feet tall and about eight inches thick. These would make perfect overhead cover for our foxholes.

Everyone started chopping down these trees to bring back to their positions. There had to be about fifty guys chopping down at least four trees each.

We started to hear yelling coming from somewhere and it was in Vietnamese. In the distance a man was running toward us with his arms waving and yelling something.

At first we thought he was some nut attacking us, but he turned out to be the owner of the land. It seems the land was a rubber plantation and these were his prize rubber trees.

We quickly finished chopping the trees we were working on and moved the logs to our positions. Someone said each tree was worth around $500, but we figured our lives were worth a bit more than that.

R&R

I was notified that I was to be going on R & R (Rest & Recuperation). That was a welcome relief after eight months in this hellhole. I had a choice of several places. In the end I chose Bangkok, Thailand.

I heard that Bangkok was the place to go, that the women were beautiful, half Asian and half French and the nightclubs are wild.

When my plane landed in Bangkok we were taken to a building at the airport and given instructions on how to act and what to expect. After a short while we were loaded onto busses and left the airport heading downtown to our assigned hotels.

Bangkok was a mix of very old traditional and very modern buildings. There were tall buildings mixed with old Buddhist Temples. It was similar to Saigon with all the bicycles, but more modern.

Away from the downtown area were the shacks and poverty that was everywhere I went while in Southeast Asia. The vendors were selling their food and anything else they could find.

When we stopped at the first hotel, a representative from the hotel came onto the bus. He was followed by a couple of the hotel's employees and they handed out quart bottles of beer to the rest of us, even though we weren't staying at their hotel. We thought that was great.

At the second hotel the same thing occurred, more beer. By the time I arrived at my hotel I was toasted, along with the rest of the bus.

I went to my room and the first thing I asked the bellboy was how much for a girl? He told me that a girl would be $11 for twenty-four hours. I told him to send me one as soon as possible.

While I was unpacking my clothes a Buck Sgt. I met on the bus came over to my room. He was nineteen years old and already made Buck Sgt. He was tall, about six feet two inches, and his name was Rabbit.

That was all he wanted to be called. He told me that he was going to the bar and to meet him there after I got settled in.

I would have been fine on my own while in Bangkok. Just being out of Vietnam for a week was good enough. Hooking up with Rabbit was going to make things a lot more interesting.

There was a knock on my door, when I opened it there was a girl sent by the bellboy. She was five feet three inches tall and had a nice figure. She was nice looking and seemed pleasant enough. I invited her in.

After I finished unpacking I heard another knock on the door. It was Rabbit and he had a bottle of vodka in one hand and two glasses in the other.

He came in the room, looked at the girl, made some kind of remark and gave me a glass. He poured some vodka in both glasses and made a toast to the two of us. Something about still being alive, and then we drank them down. As soon as the drinks were gone he poured another drink.

Now I never was much of a drinker, but being in Bangkok for only one week and then having to go back to Vietnam I decided to go for it. I downed the second drink and was feeling dizzy. Between the beer on the bus and now the vodka, I was wasted.

The girl started complaining about my drinking. After a few minutes of her complaining I threw her out. I called the front desk and asked for another girl.

A little while later another girl arrived. I have no idea what she looked like. Hell, at that point I had no idea what I looked like. It was nearing the end of the night.

Rabbit and I started trading stories, which included a lot of cursing. Every other word was a curse word and before long the second girl started to complain. After a few minutes of her complaining I threw her out.

Two girls, $22, and still no action. I'd better behave. I was able to find the phone after a short search. It was right where it had always been, but I was having difficulty seeing. I called the front desk and asked for another girl, one with a lot of patience.

When the third girl arrived I threw Rabbit out and went to bed, to sleep.

The Waiter

The bars in Bangkok were very modern, more modern than any bars I've seen in the States. They were large and had two bands so there was continuous music, all American and good.

The dance floor was in the center of the room and surrounded by GI's.
There was the bandstand at one end of the room with an entrance to the bar next to the band.

The waiters wore black pants with white shirts. They had on red jackets and black bowties, and they all carried flashlights.

Rabbit and I sat with a few other guys we met on the bus. They were sitting in a rather large booth shaped like a horseshoe. We started talking about different things when a waiter came over and took our order.

One guy asked the waiter why they are all wearing flashlights. The waiter pointed to the girls dancing in the middle of the room. He explained that if anyone wanted a particular girl he would shine his flashlight on her and she would come over to see who wanted her. This was pretty cool.

I just happened to be wearing black pants and a white shirt. I told the others to watch this. I got up and went to the bar where the other waiters were. I told them that they don't know how to get bigger tips and that I would show them.

They laughed and said to go ahead and show them. I took the next order out to a table and when I delivered the drinks I told the GIs I needed a big tip and not to be cheap. They gave me a nice tip.

When I returned to the bar I placed the tip in the waiters tip jar. They were eager for me to take the next order. Before I went to deliver the next order I asked for a red jacket. One of the waiters quickly gave me his red jacket and off I went.

Again I returned and deposited a nice size tip and again they wanted me to do more. I asked for a bowtie and got one immediately. After making them a nice amount of money, I asked for a flashlight, which was what I was looking for.

A waiter gave me his flashlight and off I went with the order. After delivering the order I went over to my booth where the others were watching and said to get ready. I took the flashlight and started shining it on all the girls on the dance floor.

All of a sudden about fifteen girls came trotting over. I took off the jacket, bowtie and gave them, along with the flashlight and the money from the last order to another waiter standing nearby. I sat down with the rest of my group.

I had a little trouble squeezing in which in itself was cool.

Baboons

When R & R was over I returned to my platoon and it was business as usual. They were in the field so I hooked a ride with the next mess delivery.

War brings out the best and the worst in people. After moving in to a new area late in the afternoon, we dug in and prepared for the night.

At dusk a clearing patrol consisting of three to five men were sent out about seventy-five meters to patrol the perimeter.

When they returned we would have a "Turkey Shoot" where each GI unloads a magazine into the brush for several reasons. To clear anything that might be lurking out there, to become comfortable firing his weapon; and also to make sure his weapon is functioning properly.

One morning we were awakened early by a large group of baboons high up in the trees. Something must have spooked them because they were screaming and jumping back and forth along the branches.

When it came time for the morning turkey shoot some of the guys aimed up in the trees and started shooting the baboons. They started falling from the treetops, at least ten of them.

The cease-fire order was given and the CO was pissed. Only a few guys shot the baboons, but it was enough. The guys who shot them had to bury them. It was a nice change watching other guys dig a hole.

Point Man

The entire 1st battalion was to go on a search and destroy mission. Headquarters Company (recon) was to take point. My squad was assigned point. It was my turn to be the point man.

A few hundred guys walking through the jungle in an upside down "V" formation and I was the first person. To say I was a little nervous would be a huge understatement.

The jungle was thick and there was no path. I gave my rifle to a friend of mine to hang on to because I was given a shotgun and a machete.

The shotgun was for close range fire and the machete was because I had to chop my way through the brush. My biggest fear was not VC. It was snakes, especially the green mamba.

I don't know much about snakes, but I heard that the green mamba would kill a human in about three seconds. It's probably not true, but I didn't want to find out.

If we were to get ambushed by a significant size group of VC then I should be okay. They would wait until the first group of guys passed them so there would be a larger target. However, if there were only a few VC then I would be their main target.

Shoot me and stop the patrol until a medivac arrives. This was not a good situation to be in. I kept thinking about how I could be on the beach at Ft. Monmouth, sunning myself. I was a moron for not signing those papers.

After a few hours of chopping my way through the jungle I was relieved. I gave my shotgun and machete to some other guy. I got my rifle and went back a bit in line.

Perimeter Guards

Occasionally we got to guard a field base camp, artillery base, or some other stationary camp in the field. This meant we would be there for a week or more. The foxholes became bunkers, fortified with extra sandbags and logs. We only had to dig one hole for the duration of our stay so we made it strong.

On this occasion we were to guard a fire support base, artillery. We were flown in by helicopter early afternoon. The base was in a valley surrounded by hills. We dug in and had enough time to build bunkers with overhead cover and sandbags. They were nice and safe.

Around five pm the commander of the artillery base told our commander that we were too close to the artillery. If they had to fire their artillery at point blank range they would fire right into us.

We had to move further up the hill. It was getting late and when we walked up the hill the ground became very muddy. We would hear our boots squishing in the mud. The ground was soaking wet.

It was strange because at the bottom where we were it was fine, but as we moved up the hill it was getting muddier. When we reached a suitable area we started to dig our new foxholes.

As soon as we made any progress water would fill the hole. After attempting to find a spot dry enough to make a hole we finally gave up.

There was another problem going up the hill. The terrain wouldn't allow us to spread out, but rather forced us to squeeze together. Instead of having two or three men to a position, we had five.

We blew up our air mattresses and placed them next to each other on the ground. Mine was in the middle of my position. Around 10:00 pm we had incoming mortars.

I had been in several mortar attacks before but they were scattered and not near me. This time was different. The mortars were dropping right on top of us. I thought we were all goners.

Mud was flying all over us, the noise was deafening, but there was nothing we could do. Guys were yelling for the medic. I just lay on my air mattress with both hands covering my head praying. After about what seemed like an hour, but actually only a few minutes, the mortars stopped.

Recon platoon was down to nineteen men. That attack hit thirteen of them. To everyone's amazement, no one was killed. In fact no one was seriously wounded. One guy was sent back to the States only because he had little time left in country. After treating the ones with minor wounds, we were left with six guys in the platoon.

The reason we had so few serious injuries was the muddy ground. The mortars dropped a few inches below ground level before they exploded. My backpack took a direct hit, all I could think of was "Thank God I wasn't wearing it." I have been in six mortar attacks so far, but this was the worst.

The Pond

The next week, during another operation, we were on our usual patrol. The jungle was hot and there was thick brush all around. We arrived at a clearing, which was to be our destination, and began to setup.

After a while a few guys came by and said there was a pond and guys were going swimming in it. It was brutally hot and that sounded like a fantastic idea.

We finished setting up our position and a few of us started towards the pond. We came upon a pond about fifty feet long and twenty-five feet wide. It was on the side of a steep hill with thick brush behind it.

The front of the pond was clear and guys were already swimming in it while others were jumping in. It looked great and I was anxious to get in and cool off.

As we approached the pond everyone started getting out of it and running back our way. They were yelling for us to go back, but we had no idea why.

Then one guy stopped by us, turned and pointed to the hill at the end of the pond. There, slithering down the hill and into the pond was the biggest snake I ever saw in my life.

Someone said it was an Anaconda because of its size, but we weren't sure. All we knew is that the pond wasn't big enough for both of us, so we took off.

The heat wasn't that bad after that.

Grenade Follies

With only a couple of months to go in country I was becoming a short timer. I had been through six mortar attacks, a few sniper attacks, a few firefights and I was a seasoned combat veteran.

Back at base camp we received an FNG. He was a nineteen year old Buck Sgt. named Morales. He was wearing a CIB (Combat Infantry Badge) with a star in the middle, signifying multiple combat theaters. It turned out that he spent two days in the Dominican Republic.

We questioned his previous combat and even poked fun at it. He became my fire team leader. Not too cool since he had no clue. He was trying to act as if he knew what he was doing. He said all the wrong things.

When he told us to spit shine our jungle boots we laughed at him, which of course made him even madder. No one respected him and he knew it.

He would complain to the Platoon Sergeant but the Platoon Sergeant wouldn't back him up because he knew he was getting too carried away with his new rank.

After a few weeks with this FNG, Sgt. Morales, we were on an operation. While hanging around my foxhole with nothing to do, I started playing around with a grenade. I knew how they were constructed and I was curious to see the inside.

I unscrewed the top and removed the detonator. Then I dumped the gunpowder out on the ground. After it was safe, I removed the pin and took the handle off.

When I had it completely apart I started to reassemble it, minus the gun powder and the detonator. I screwed the top back on and placed the handle in position and was about to reinsert the pin.

About this time Sgt. Morales walked up and asked me what I was doing. I told him I was trying to get the pin back into the grenade. Once he realized what I was doing he started to panic.

Instead of telling him the grenade was safe, I began to act as though he was making me nervous. This got him going. He started yelling at me to put the pin in over and over.

I told him it wouldn't go in and made like I was panicking. I kept trying to get the pin in the grenade but wasn't able to.

By this time a few other guys who saw me taking the grenade apart were watching, waiting to see what was next.

After he yelled some more I took the grenade, with the pin out and threw it at him yelling, "You do it." When I threw the grenade the handle flew off and Sgt. Morales hit the ground.

We all just sat there laughing at him. When he realized what I did, he jumped up and ordered me to drop and do twenty-five push-ups. I just looked at him and laughed.

He went to the platoon Sgt. and told him what happened. The platoon Sgt. talked to him for a few minutes and that was the end of it. Sgt. Morales didn't bother us with any more stateside bullshit.

My Last Operation

The last operation I was to be on in Vietnam was Operation Junction City, Feb. 22, 1967. The operation began with the first combat jump since the Korean War. The jump was to be made by the 2nd Battalion, 173rd Airborne.

When we began we were told that we would be guarding the base camp. However we would also be carrying on daily operations such as patrols and night ambushes.

We arrived at the location assigned to us and started digging in. There were to be twelve positions with two men in each position. I was in position with Pvt. Del Kloog, from Chicago.

I took out my entrenching tool and hit the ground. It was like a rock, all you could hear was the sound of "clink, clink" I wasn't going anywhere with this ground. I threw down my entrenching tool and told Del that the ground was too hard to dig.

He took my entrenching tool and tried himself. Having the same results we looked for other alternatives.

While in the jungle or at base camp most of the time spent is sitting around waiting for something. One of the more popular things to do is to play cards. We played hearts, spades, and a few other games.

We played for money, usually a dollar a point. If we were in the field we had to wait for payday to get paid. This was our pastime and Pvt. Baker owed me $148.

I was going back to base camp in a few weeks and leaving Vietnam, and the army. My two years were up and I was going home.

Pvt. Baker didn't know this and that was good. He would not have to pay me the money he owed me because the rest of the unit was going to stay in the field long after I was gone.

I went over to Pvt. Baker who was finishing up his hole and made him an offer. Dig my foxhole and we'll call the debt paid. He jumped on it because I would have taken all his pay. This way he'd get to keep his money.

He started digging. He was a big, strong farm boy and was used to hard work. All we heard was "clink, clink, clink" over and over again. After about three hours Pvt. Baker had enough.

The hole was about two feet wide, four feet long and about three feet deep, just enough for me and Del to get below ground level. He would finish the hole the next day.

Del and I set up a hammock behind our position. That night we were to take turns standing guard. He was on duty until midnight. Then it would be my turn until morning.

It was 10:30 at night when Del shook me in the hammock. "Incoming", he yelled and pulled me from my sleep. I jumped into the foxhole with Del and got down.

During the next minutes, mortars started dropping all around us. All the foxholes had sandbags with logs on top of them and more sandbags on top of the logs, all but us; we had a hole, three feet deep. The mortars kept coming, more and more. They knew exactly where we were.

We could hear the loud whistle and then the loudest sound I ever heard in my life. There would be a loud "crack" sound along with a bright white flash of light. They were hitting right by us. Every time a mortar dropped it sent dirt flying over us. We were pretty much covered with dirt after the first few mortars dropped.

I thought for sure we were going to take a direct hit. They say that there are no atheists in foxholes. This is true, I was praying as fast as I could. I kept my head down all the time, but every once in a while, Del would stick his head up to see if we were going to be attacked.

I just stayed down, praying harder and harder.

When the attack finished, our weapons platoon started firing mortars back at them. They would fire flares to light up the area so we could see what was out there. While a steady barrage of flares was being set off, a few of us started playing cards.

I don't think anyone kept track of who was winning. We were all so scared that this was a way to get through it. We were laughing at how stupid this must seem, but it did the trick.

The next morning we found out that every foxhole took a direct hit, everyone but ours. At first we thought it was because ours wasn't built up like the others, then we looked and saw the freakiest thing I've seen yet.

There were five holes, where mortar rounds fell, within three feet of the edge of our hole.

That day, we, along with everyone else, created the most fortified foxholes we ever had.

I had a few weeks left.

The Brown Heart

When a soldier is wounded in combat he is awarded a Purple Heart. This signifies that he sustained wounds from the enemy while in the service of his country.

The second week of Operation Junction City I was assigned to go on a clearing patrol at dusk. There were four of us and we only had to go across our twelve positions, a quick trip.

We started out at my end of the perimeter and went out about seventy-five meters and then turn and patrol in front of our perimeter. Everything was quiet.

Then we heard some mortars. At first we thought they were outgoing. Then we quickly realized they were incoming. By this time we were at the other end of the perimeter.

We started running in, yelling "Rawhide" the running password (Vietnamese pronounce it "Lawhide). As we were running we were setting off trip flares.

Mortars were dropping all around us, in front of and behind us. It was getting bad, just like the last attack. By this time we were getting close to our line. Now I had to get to my foxhole.

There were too many mortars dropping, I didn't have time to get there, so I decided to go into the closest bunker.

The guy ahead of me was heading towards a bunker. It had an opening at the back that would allow you to jump right in. He jumped, feet first into the opening and disappeared. I followed him into the hole. I started to jump into the bunker when a mortar round hit directly behind me and I was hit in the middle of my back.

It hit hard and I knew what it meant. I was wounded. How bad I didn't know, but I knew I was hit. It felt like someone hit me in the middle of my back as hard as they could with a baseball bat.

I landed in the bunker and moved away from the opening. I just stood there, not moving, I thought I may already be dead and this is what it was like.

I tapped on the shoulder of the Pvt. who was ahead of me and asked, "Am I talking?" He turned and looked at me and said, "What?" Again I asked him if I was talking. He said I was and wanted to know why I asked.

At that time I reached behind me as best I could and felt around my back. In the middle, where I was hit it was wet and hot…blood.

I was scared that I had sustained a severe wound and although I was conscious, I was thinking that the reason I didn't feel bad was because I was going into shock.

I told the other Pvt. that I think I was hit in the back. He told me to turn around and he would take a look at it. I turned around and with his lighter he looked at my back. I felt him touching it and thinking, "why doesn't it hurt?"

He turned me back, facing him, and said, "You're hit alright, with mud, hot mud." He held his finger up in the light and showed me the mud. Somehow, when the mortar exploded behind me, the shrapnel went around me and only mud from the explosion hit me.

I always felt the army should have awarded a "Brown Heart"… not for the mud.

My Last Mission

April 30, 1967 was my last day in the jungle. I was heading back to base camp the next day and processing out of Vietnam and the army.

It was past my two years of required service and I also completed the extra time to make up from the stockade. I was heading home, well, not quite.

Recon platoon was ordered to send a squad out to set up a night ambush. We were to go out about five hundred meters and set up the ambush.

This was a common task for us. One we did often. There were eight of us, a Sgt. who was the squad leader, a medic; I was the RTO, and five riflemen. We left around 4:00 pm.

The jungle was thick and it was hot and humid. I was more nervous than usual because on this operation we already sustained two heavy mortar attacks, both coming extremely close to me. I felt I was lucky so far, but my luck couldn't last forever.

There was enemy activity in the area. We heard about different incidents and were on alert for anything. I was going in the next day. I kept thinking "I shouldn't be out here."

My radio antenna was catching on to everything, even though my radio's 8 foot antenna was folded in half. The humidity was unbearable and the air was heavy. It was getting dark from the clouds overhead. I felt like this whole operation was wrong.

It just didn't feel right. We were going out with an FNG on his first operation and two guys leaving Vietnam the next day, Pvt. James Chronister and me.

We arrived at a small clearing along a path and the Sgt. gave the word to set up. The Sgt., the medic, and I set up position in the center, while the five riflemen set up in a circle around us.

The riflemen were about ten feet from the center. Once we set up it started to get dark and all activity came to a halt.

To be successful in an ambush you had to be still and quiet. There was absolutely no talking, smoking, or anything else that may give away your position.

If you violated any of these rules you could get shot or you could get your buddies shot. This was a hard and fast rule.

After a few hours of nothing, it started to rain. It had been building up all afternoon. The clouds were getting darker and darker, and then they unloaded on us.

It was a downpour like we have encountered many times before in Vietnam. One I was not going to miss when I got back to the "World".

It started raining at exactly 9:23 pm. I know it because I kept checking my watch to see when we were going to be done so I could get out of this God forsaken country.

At about 11:05 pm something started crawling up my left leg inside my pants. I had no idea what it was but it kept climbing higher. Whatever it was it was small, about an inch or two.

My first thought was a snake, a green mamba. Then I realized it was too small. I thought it might be a leech; those things can get into anything. I reached down and caught whatever it was between my fingers and started to squeeze, keeping quiet all the time.

I had the thing trapped by my knee and kept squeezing it. I was afraid to let go just in case it wasn't dead. Then, out of nowhere, we heard a single gunshot. I looked at my watch and it was 11:31 pm.

Everyone froze. Because of the close proximity, we didn't know if the gunshot was incoming or outgoing. Afterwards there was no sound other than the rain falling. No one slept, we just waited.

Morning came and everything seemed okay. The Sgt., medic, and I were getting our gear ready to go back to our unit. One of the other riflemen came over to the medic and told him that Pvt. Chronister wouldn't wake up.

The medic went to see what the problem was. A few minutes later he returned to inform the Sgt. that Pvt. Chronister was shot and killed.   He had been shot in the face at close range.

Pvt. Chronister's body was lying by the FNG; he had been lying there for over six hours. According to the FNG, he was sitting up against a tree with his rifle in his hand. He heard a noise and saw someone walking up to his position.

It was dark and he couldn't make out who it was. The person walking went right up to the FNG's position and stood right in front of him. The FNG said he asked "Who is there?" twice and got no response.

He pointed his rifle and fired a single shot. He heard a body drop and froze. In the morning, when he realized he had shot one of us, he was devastated.

The only explanation of why Pvt. Chronister walked over to the new guy was to scare him. To, "welcome him to the jungle." He had done similar things before with other guys. This time it cost him his life.

The jungle was too thick for a helicopter. It was even too thick to drop a line. We had to carry Pvt. Chronister back with us. Everyone took turns carrying him and no one complained about it.

It was one thing to hear about someone dying, or even to see the body of a fallen soldier, but to carry a comrade, a friend, a buddy back, especially through the thick jungle was too much for some to bear.

A couple of guys vomited. We did the things people do when

someone you know dies. I kept thinking how he was going in with me today to process out of the country. How close he was to freedom.

The walk back to camp was long and slow. It took most of the morning to go five hundred meters. My antennae caught onto everything again and it seemed more frustrating than on the way out.

We carried Pvt. Chronister the best we could. One man was in back of him holding his legs, while two men were in front holding each arm. He was gone, but we carried him as if he wasn't.

The thing that sticks in my head the most when carrying Pvt. Chronister back was that he was face up and I had his right arm. He was shot at point blank right in the face. Most of his face was gone leaving a crater where his mouth and nose would be.

He was dead for over six hours. His face was covered in blood which had turned purple and black during the night. As I carried him through the jungle I kept looking at his face. That image is burned into my head and I will never forget it.

When we finally returned to our unit Pvt. Chronister was placed in a body bag and loaded on a helicopter.

As planned, Pvt. Chronister and I went back to base camp at Bien Hoa together.

Going Home

When we returned to Bien Hoa Pvt. Chronister was taken by ambulance to the base hospital. I went back to my barracks and gathered up my belongings preparing to leave Vietnam. I couldn't wait to get out of there.

It was still morning when I was transported to Camp Alpha for processing. Camp Alpha was near Saigon and was the main processing center for everyone in our area leaving Vietnam.

When I got there, I was grouped with others leaving the same time I was. We were told where to be and at what time to be there, no problem. All I had to remember was to report to a specific tent at 9:00 pm.

There we would walk over to a building for final clearance. At 2:00 am we would be loaded onto a truck and driven to Bien Hoa airbase for our flight home.

Everything was set, by this time tomorrow I would be drinking a beer in the good old US of A. "Freedom bird, here I come."

While waiting for 9:00 pm to roll around, I decided to go to the enlisted men's club to have a beer to celebrate my successful completion of my tour in Vietnam.

Once there I ran into a sailor. We hit it off right away and had a few beers while talking. This was not a good idea.

He told me he was going home on standby. The reason he was going home on standby was because he had missed his flight, actually, five flights. All the while we were talking he kept buying more beers.

When I asked him why he missed his flight, he told me that he keeps getting drunk and passing out. I thought, "What an idiot, how could anyone be stupid enough to miss their flight going home because they were drunk."

It was time for mess and I was feeling pretty toasted myself. After mess I decided to go to the meeting tent and wait there.

It was around 7:00 pm and there were only a couple of hours to go, and it was raining. I had about five beers, which was about four beers too many, and was getting tired.

I grabbed my duffle bag and proceeded to the meeting tent. When I got there I found the tent completely empty. There was nothing at all in the tent. The floor was concrete and it was wet. I was hoping to sleep on the floor using my duffle bag as a pillow, but that was impossible.

Then another guy walked in the tent. He also was leaving that night. I started talking to him and he told me he wasn't moving from that tent for any reason. He was out of there and nothing was going to stop him.

I told him the tent next door was empty and had cots in it. I said I needed to lie down and if I went there would he wake me when 8:30 rolled around. I told him I would be in the first bunk. He agreed and I went and lay down.

I woke up a little while later and decided to go back to the meeting tent. When I got there it was still empty. Only this time the guy I met was gone also.

I looked at my watch, 2:00 am, "SHIT, he never woke me up!" I ran to the building where we were to go and I was informed that the truck to Bien Hoa left a few minutes ago.

There was nothing I could do; I would have to go standby, like the sailor.

Standby

The next day I was walking around the compound and saw the sailor. I asked him why he was still there and he told me he got drunk again and missed his flight. He asked me if I wanted to get a beer and I said, "Fuck no! What are you crazy?"

He laughed and said yes. I asked him if he wanted to go home because it didn't seem like he was trying too hard. He told me that he was bored and the only thing to do was to drink.

We stayed together, waiting for the next flight that had standby seats. Three days later we both were informed there were seats available.

That night we were included with the group heading for Bien Hoa.

When we arrived at the airbase, the standbys had to wait in a separate area. There were four seats available for standby and there were five of us. Top priority was a Pvt. who volunteered to extend his tour another six months giving him a special thirty-day leave.

Next priority was a Colonel, next was a Major. Fourth priority was the sailor and I was last. The standbys were told not to worry. There would be another flight out thirty minutes later. The only problem was that there were more standbys coming.

Things didn't look good for me.

I didn't know what to do. I could ask someone to give me his seat but that would be dreaming.

The sailor had to get out of there. Hell, he never got this close to the airbase and who knew how long it would take to get back. The officers wouldn't even talk to anyone but each other. The only chance I had was to get the Pvt. on special leave to give me his seat.

I explained to the Pvt. how he had top priority on this flight. He knew there would be another flight just thirty minutes later. It would be absolutely no problem to get on the next flight.

He would still have top priority over everyone. At first he said no. After a while, I convinced him to let me have his seat. I wish I knew who he was. I would have liked to return the favor someday.

Freedom Bird

There were approximately three hundred seats on the plane. The airline was Continental Airlines. There were no "classes". Everyone flew in the same class, coach.

I figured they made as many seats available as possible. We started to board with me being the last on the plane.

When I walked into the cabin I saw the only seat left. It was in the front row, on the right side, center seat, between the Colonel and the Major. I sat down and said, "Hi" to the officers.

They both turned their heads and looked at me, and then they turned back, never saying a word. I thought to myself, "Officers, and leg officers at that. Fuck'em." I buckled up, put the headphones, which were on my seat, on my head and sat back.

I searched the audio channel for something I was familiar with until I found one. It was a couple of Beatles songs. I sat back, closed my eyes, and listened to "Penny Lane" and "Strawberry Fields" for the entire eighteen hour flight home. The only interruption was meal time and a couple of trips to the bathroom.

Behind me were the rest of the troops having a great time, hollering and singing and doing everything and anything they wanted.

We were in the air forever, but that was ok. The trip to Vietnam on the ship took eighteen days. The trip back home took eighteen hours, a fair ratio.

After what seemed like an eternity the captain came on over the speakers. He told us that we were nearing the coast of California and that we should be able to see it soon.

The yelling slowed down a lot, but there was still a lot of talking.

Everyone was looking out the windows. All of a sudden someone shouted, "There it is!" The whole plane went crazy. We could see the coastline. We were home. Everyone was yelling and shouting like before, except this time it was cheers of joy, not ranking or anything like that.

A short while later the Captain came back on the PA. He told us to fasten our seatbelts and place our seats and tray tables in an upright position. We are going in for our final descent. We were landing at Travis Air Force Base.

The airplane was now quiet. Not a word was said and some guys started crying. We were descending lower and lower. The lights outside were getting bigger and brighter. We were getting real close. There wasn't a sound on the plane. It was eerily quiet.

As the plane got closer and lower, all eyes were glued to the windows. Lower and lower. It seemed like it was taking forever. Then we felt a slight bump and heard the tires screech when they hit the ground.

All hell broke loose in the airplane. Everyone started yelling and screaming. Many were crying openly. Nobody cared. We were home at last.

The captain came back on the speakers and the first thing he said was, "Welcome home boys" followed with the usual instructions to stay seated, etc.

We didn't pull up to a gate. Instead a stairway was brought up to the plane. When the door was opened the first person to deplane was the colonel, followed by the major. I was next. Standing in the doorway, the colonel stopped and said, "Oh, it's cold out here."

Not caring who was holding up the line, everyone shouted, "MOVE" and pushed their way out the door. The colonel got the message right away and hurried out the door and down the stairway.

Everyone got off the plane and was exuberant. Some were hugging each other while others dropped to their knees and prayed for thanks. Still others got down and kissed the ground.

This was a time for celebration. We returned to the United States after our tour of duty was complete.

I couldn't help think about the ones who didn't make it back. Ray Lofton, Frank Smith, Jim Chronister and all the others, some who I knew and the thousands I didn't.

How did it affect their families? Did they have children or wives? I thought of all the mothers and fathers who lost a son or daughter. I was happy to be home. It was a bittersweet feeling.

Oakland Army Terminal

We landed at Travis Air Force Base and were loaded onto buses and taken to Oakland Army Terminal for processing. We arrived 6:00 am, exactly four hours after take-off, only in a different time zone.

The flight was eighteen hours, non-stop. As we drove along the highway the simplest things became things of beauty. Roads for instance, it had been almost a year since I'd seen a paved road.

Buildings more than one story high and not made of straw and mud, automobiles, with women in them. These all looked fantastic.

The drive back to Oakland was the beginning of our healing process. We were starting to get used to the familiar surroundings. We arrived at the terminal around 8:00 am.

Most of the guys returning were directed a different way than myself and a few others. I was getting out of the army, finished, complete, and adios MF.

I was given a physical, a new dress uniform, complete with the 173rd patch on my left shoulder signifying my last unit, and a 173rd patch on my right shoulder signifying my combat unit. I received a "Recon" patch to go over it.

I also received the most important thing of all, my "Combat Infantry Badge", which, along with my jump wings were the only two things I cared about.

My process out of the service took all day. I remember calling home and telling them I would probably get home sometime tomorrow. I was discharged at around 9:00 pm.

I grabbed a cab outside and headed to San Francisco airport. I was going home.

At the airport I looked to get on the next plane headed to JFK, LaGuardia, or Newark airport, it didn't matter. I got on a flight to JFK airport. It was to land in NY around 5:00 am.

I was wearing my new dress uniform and was looking good. At the airport I was a little concerned because I heard that some assholes actually spit on soldiers returning from Vietnam.

I could not imagine why anyone would do that.

Taxi to NJ

When I arrived at JFK I immediately went outside and got into the first cab. I asked the driver how much it would cost to go to Little Falls, NJ. He looked it up and said $20. I agreed and we took off.

As we drove he started asking me questions about my service. I told him I was returning from Vietnam and I hadn't been home in a year.

He didn't ask the usual stupid questions like "Did you kill anyone" or things like that. He asked my opinion of the war. We had a nice conversation all the way to Little Falls.

He asked if I was in the Air Force because my patch said "Airborne", and I explained. He was impressed.

When we got close to my home I asked him to let me off on the corner of Main Street and Route 23. This was about a half-mile from my house and I wanted to walk it. I got out of the cab and went to give him his $20.

He told me, "Forget it. Welcome home." This was the reaction of everyone I met. They were supportive and appreciative. I thanked him and off I went.

It was around 6:00 am, May 7th. The weather was clear and cool. I threw my duffle bag over my shoulder and started walking. I wanted to take my time and just look at all the things I took for granted growing up.

A guy pulled up and stopped to offer me a ride. I explained how I just wanted to walk.

He said, "Welcome home and thanks".

I walked past my old grammar school, School #3, Little Falls. Past my aunt and uncle's house, my grandmother's street, and several more familiar places.

It was unlike any other time in my life. I Felt like I was in heaven.

Then I turned the bend and saw my home. I could feel the swelling in my chest. My eyes started to tear. I was almost home.

Home Sweet Home

I arrived home at 6:30 AM. I walked to my house and from the front sidewalk I yelled for everyone to wake up. I walked up to the door and started ringing the doorbell, over and over. After a minute or two the door opened. It was my mother.

She took one look at me and started to cry, at which point I got choked up also, I was teary eyed the whole walk home.

We hugged for a while, I don't think she ever wanted to let go and that was fine with me, my Dad walked in and we also hugged for a while.

My brother Bill and sister Jo both came in the room and after all the hugging and kissing was complete they all said the same thing, "You look so skinny, what happened?"

When I left for Vietnam a year earlier, I weighed 180 pounds with very little fat on me. When I got on the scale after I returned home I weighed 140 pounds. I lost 40 pounds in the year I was gone. Mom got out all her pots and pans and started cooking, in a few months I was back up to 180.

I still remember the look in my brother's eyes, he was still my big brother, the college graduate, but this time he looked at me a little different, and that was good. There was a respect that words can't describe.

I was home.

EPILOG

Fulfilling the Vow

In June of 1980, I was on a business trip to San Jose, California. I was with my computer representative, Patty Molet. I was going to school to be trained on a new computer my company was acquiring.

I was going to be gone for one week. Each day was filled with classes.
However, on Wednesday we were told we had half a day to do whatever we wanted.

My rep said a few people were going to drive to San Francisco for the rest of the day and be back later and would I like to join them. I said I would like it and the two of us took off for San Francisco.

On the sixty-mile drive from San Jose to San Francisco we spoke about many things. Mainly the computer system I was getting. But then I started thinking about something else.

I started thinking about the trip to Vietnam. It had been fourteen years since I made that vow on the ship. I couldn't get it out of my mind. I wanted to see the Golden Gate Bridge. I wanted to drive over it.

It was all I could think about, but could I tell her about it without sounding like a wimp? She wouldn't understand.

Finally, after several minutes of thinking about it, I asked her if she would mind driving across the bridge. She said sure, but why? So, without making myself look like a pansy, I briefly told her about the vow a bunch of us made.

I remember seeing the bridge and everything started coming back. We drove across to the other side of the bridge.

There was a small park there and I asked her to pull in. I got out and walked away from the car to get a better view of the bridge. I stood there for a while, thinking about that year, the worst year of my life.

I thought about the fifty-eight thousand young men who didn't make it, about Pvt. Lofton, Pvt. Smith, and Pvt. Chronister.

By this time I was getting choked up.

I stood at attention and saluted the bridge. I completed my vow.

On the way back I started to explain, but Patty cut me off and said, "You don't have to explain anything. Welcome home soldier".

The Wall

In the summer of 1983, I was traveling with my family to visit my brother and his family in Atlanta. We were going to go around Washington, D.C.

I decided to take a shortcut right through the center of Washington and stop by the newly built Vietnam Veterans Memorial, the "Wall."

I heard about it and saw pictures of it, but I never went there. This was my opportunity.

When we arrived, I was a little nervous. I didn't want to appear like a wimp to my family. I found the sections I needed to know and started my search.

I found Ray Lofton. I stood there and everything that happened that day came back in detail, it wasn't hard to remember, I already thought about him every day.

I found Frank Smith and thought it could have been me up there on the "Wall".

And finally, I saw the name of Jim Chronister.

I said some prayers for them and for the 58,000 other men and women who never made it back alive.

Then for the very last time I stood at attention and saluted the "Wall"